Sign's Up

By
Vick Vickery

Good Sign Publishing Company
Pensacola, Florida

Seventh Edition
September 1995

COVER PICTURE:
Eagle Scout
Wayne Lee Bowman Jr.
Little Rock, AR 1977

Copyright © 1988 By Vick Vickery

Publisher:
Good Sign Publishing Co.
4195 April Road
Pensacola, Florida 32504

Library of Congress Catalog No.: 88-80454
ISBN 0-9620202-0-6

Catalog No.: BSA 34080

To
The Memory of O.B. "Country" Gorman

A great story teller who was a living parable of the Scout Oath and Law.

From one of "Country's boys"

A Scout Salute

The stories recorded in SIGN'S UP have all been taken directly from performances on "the stage of life." With gratitude, I recognize the actors, stage hands and recorders who have helped produce these vignettes of comedy and character.

Thank you, *actors* — Scouts and leaders, funny and serious, rehearsed and unrehearsed. Your lines have been the inspiration and application for these parables.

Thank you, *recorders* — you helped us preserve these acts in pictures and words. Many of the stories would have been lost somewhere in a camp-fire, church basement, creek bank, or perhaps on a mountain top, had it not been for your vision and memory.

Thank you, *my loving family*, for your support and encouragement.

Thank you, Joe Pete McNeil, for your technical help in producing this book.

Thank you, to the Boy Scouts of America for allowing me to reprint some of the images of Scouting from my first handbook, the 1938 edition of *The Handbook for Boys*. These early images stirred in me a lasting enchantment with Scouting. May they rekindle in you that same exciting Spirit.

Chapter One • SIGNS OF DIRECTION
Who Put Him In Your Wagon? 10 • Commitment Beyond the Front Porch 11 • Interior Decorator 12 • The Master's Work 13 • Sheepshank 14 • If You Can Take It 15 • A Salute To Mason 16 • Ten of What? 17 • Bugler Sound Off! 18 • Carry A Big Stick 19 • Goodwill 20 • Rare, Medium or Well Done? 21 • Hooked And Didn't Know It 22 • Poison Ivy, Easy To Spot 23 • This One Channel 24

Chapter Two • SIGNS OF LIFE
Breathe Normally 26 • On Falling 27 • Important Measurements 28 • Mistakes We Can't Cover 29 • The Heart Of A Friend 30 • Pitching In The Dark 31 • Ever Make A Heart Map? 32 • Hidden Power 33 • The Breath of Life 34 • The Living Circle 35 • Learning The "Together Stroke" 36 • Up Is Different From Down 37 • New Snakebite Treatment 38

Chapter Three • NATURE'S SIGNS
Does This Rock Your Conscience? 40 • Sure Is A Good Day To Make A Garden 41 • On "Seeds" 42 • Love The Wild Mulberries 43 • Whistle While You Work 44 • A Pigeon Scout 45 • How Many Feathers Does A Seagull Have? 46 • Let's Celebrate 47 The Middle Tree 48 • You Can Be A Giant Killer 49 • If The Creek Don't Rise 50

Chapter Four • SIGNS OF THE TIMES
Happy New Year 52 • Prepared For Today 53 • A Backward Glance 54 • I Can't Say It 55 • It Can't Be Unstuffed 56 • Getting On To The Good Part 57 • Letter From A Clown 58 • Not Without Getting Wet 59 • The Three Boys 60 • The Eight Minute Mile 61 • No Scaled Down Version 62 • Well Done 63 Full Service Management 64 • On Mixing Cement 65 • Time Release 66

Chapter Five • DANGER SIGNS
A Rescue Knot 68 • Someone Removed The Stop Sign 69 Weather People 70 • Warnings, Dangers And Risks 71 • Automatic Bailers 72 • When The Heat Is On 73 • In A Hole? • 74 The 13th Floor 75 • A Little Explosive Properly Applied 76 • Implosion 77 • Let's Make A Point 78 • Could You Be Last? 79 • Protection That Lasts 80

Chapter Six • TRAIL SIGNS
Fly Over Or The Right Stuff? 82 • Keep 'Em Burning 83 • John Jacob Jingleheimer Schmidt 84 • Navigational Instincts 85 Leadership...Lost And Found 86 • Little Things Communicate 87 • Space Listening 88 • Feet And Legs 89 • A Pain In The Toe 90 • What's Cooking? 91 • Have You Been Shortsheeted Lately? 92 • Scouting Is A Turn Off 93 • No Trace 94

Foreword

From "Strengthen the Arm of Liberty" to "Values That Last a Lifetime," I have, over the past several decades, been challenged to make my way in life by the trail signs of Scouting.

As a boy I was moved by their simplicity and idealism. I wanted to be a Scout who was, trustworthy, loyal, helpful — it didn't take long to learn to repeat the words. Why should it then, have taken so long to learn about living them?

When I became a leader I found myself responsible for marking trails for others. The bent twigs, stacked stones, and twisted grass pictured in my *Handbook for Boys*, were signs simple enough to master.

But how can a leader make clear signs for those who might follow? Can they be made from the material of the Scout Oath and Law? I think surely, therein is a rich source from which to lay the trail signs for living. They point us first to God, then to others, and finally to ourselves.

Sign's Up! By giving attention to the living signs preserved in these parables one might well discover a sign pointing him to a right turn in life. To that end this trail is laid.

Scout Sign,

Vick Vickery

This picture from the early pages of my *1938 Boy Scout Handbook*, inprinted in my mind a lasting image of what the character of a Scout should truly be. The following stories are reflections of that image.

Vick Vickery

CHAPTER ONE
Signs of Direction

Who Put Him In Your Wagon?   10

Commitment Beyond the Front Porch   11

Interior Decorator   12

The Master's Work   13

Sheepshank   14

If You Can Take It   15

A Salute To Mason   16

Ten of What?   17

Bugler Sound Off!   18

Carry A Big Stick   19

Goodwill   20

Rare, Medium or Well Done?   21

Hooked and Didn't Know It   22

Poison Ivy, Easy To Spot   23

This One Channel   24

Who Put Him in Your Wagon?

Some of my favorite times are spent talking with ol' timers about pages from the past. Youthful pranks seem to have an unchallenged position in man's aging brain cells. Apparently, they respond to rapid recalls when other life-changing events fall between the cracks. An aging friend of mine recalls a summertime "protracted" meeting in the country church where his family worshipped.

It was a custom for the smaller children to be bedded down on pallets in the backs of their family wagons while the adults shared in the evening worship. Teenage children were given the responsibility for looking after the small fry as they slept. What can be less exciting to a teenager than watching after a sleeping child?

After all the lambs were sound asleep, some enterprising older brother came up with the idea of a game of "musical children." In this case, it involved exchanging the sleeping lambs from one wagon to another.

Services over, the horse drawn wagons all headed for homes in the hills with their precious cargoes of Moms, Dads, and the lambs. Without telephone, C.B., or pickup trucks, that small community soon took on the image of a picnic in a wind storm. Needless to say, the storm didn't settle until well after sun-up the next morning.

I have always wondered how those mom's felt when they looked into their bundle to discover a goat in place of their little lamb. I suppose they were not unlike that parent today who accepts responsibility as a Den Mother or a Scoutmaster so their son can enjoy the program. Then in the first Den Meeting or first Campout, they discover they have someone else's kids. Kids, not at all like theirs, but still they are kids who have that need for love and time from adults who care.

Who put them in your wagon anyway? I think, truly, God did. He knew you have the care and love to share your time and touch with these precious young lives. Just love them as if they were yours lambs.

Commitment Beyond the Front Porch

Have you ever heard a front porch being knocked off of a house? It makes quite a sound, especially in the middle of the night. I heard this loud crash-crunch combination when I was walking back from visiting a neighbor. Immediately, I ran across the alley, up to the next street. A small car was backing away from a demolished front porch. The car stopped at the curb and a young lady got out, checking herself and her car for damages. I said, "Are you hurt?" She replied, "I don't think so." Then I asked, "Can I help you?" She looked directly at me with a most plaintiff expression and said, "Will you go in this house with me and help me tell these people I knocked their front porch off?"

Well, I had asked, "Can I help," but I really wasn't thinking of that much involvement. With the commitment already made, I said yes and walked up the pile of boards with her to the front door. It was hardly necessary to ring the bell. We were greeted by some wide-eyed, irrate occupants. After considerable discussion which ranged from, do you have insurance, to where is your bathroom, we came to calmer moments and a temporary resolution.

When we join Scouting as a volunteer, we say in fact, "Can I help?" The answer obviously is yes, but just how far does our commitment go? For many volunteers, it goes a long, long way. I never cease to be amazed at the depth of involvement of our strong volunteer leaders.

We all know that the youth in Scouting don't need our help only when it is fun and games. Often, they need us most when they have just knocked off someone's front porch. Can they count on us to walk with them through the rubble and to start them on the right steps toward healing?

"The Interior Decorator"

This summer while visiting in Sacramento, our family decided to tour the California Governor's mansion. It was built in 1887, a 15-room, 5-bath mansion of Victorian-Gothic architecture.

Nearly every room of the mansion contains a fireplace which is set with beautiful Italian marble mantels. As the tour guide described the furnishings and history of each elegant room, she also described the family and lifestyle of many of the California governors who have lived there.

When we came to the formal dining room, we were shown the silver and china patterns. A description was given of each accessory, from punch bowl to chandelier.

Pointing to the exquisite brown marble mantel, the guide said, "This mantel is back to its original beauty."

In 1911 Governor Hiram Johnson's wife decided to redecorate the dining room. She called in the finest interior decorator she could find from San Francisco. In that period, there was a popular trend toward the use of battleship grey for interior color. So.....you guessed it, Mrs. Johnson had the dining room, in its entirety, painted battleship grey. No more of that outdated Italian marble look. Fortunately, subsequent renovations have included release of the beautiful walls, ceiling and mantel from their imprisonment of battleship grey.

Have you ever thought of your work with youth as that of an "interior decorator?" You are a specialist. Your experience gained through the challenging steps of maturing has taught you much about life's colors. You know the blue of disappointment, the red of caution, the golden yellow of friendship, the green of growing.

You have been chosen not just as a decorator, but an interior decorator. Your most important task is to help young people see in themselves the beauty which God has placed there. To strengthen their commitment, not to cover up or destroy it with some trendy color foisted on them by the crowd. What you help them preserve, no one will have to help restore.

The Masters Work

The most valuable of all violins are some made by Antonio Stradivari between 1670 and 1737. Everyone has heard of a Stradivari violin. His name is synonymous with quality and value in violins, but why are his violins so valuable? Is it tone? I was surprised to learn that there is a Stradivari violin in existence which is known as, "The Violin the Master Forgot to Burn." It has been the despair of many experts because of the impossibility of getting a good tone out of this instrument. It is valuable as a rare execption. Are Stradivari violins valuable because there are so few made? Not so. There are over two hundred fifty violins known to be works of the master.

Why should a non-musical person such as I fiddle with such trivia? A friend recently gave me an old Etude Music Magazine printed in June, 1941. The front cover pictured a Scout playing a bugle. I read these interesting facts in an article entitled, "Paradox of the Violin." In reading about the "Violin the Master Forgot to Burn," I began remembering some Scouts I have known in camp and in various Scouting events over the years. The only clues to their being Scouts were their uniforms and registration cards. They did not speak like Scouts, look like Scouts or act like Scouts. Their whole tone was foreign to that which Scouting sought to instill in them. Thank goodness the Scoutmaster forgot to "burn" them. Unbeknowing to them, their Scoutmaster's workmanship was somehow shaping the framework of character which would one day become a man of great worth to his church, family and community. Today I look upon them in amazement when I consider the toneless days of their youth.

Scouts from past years are valuable today as leaders not because they have been so few. Over 60 million have been members of the Scouting movement in the United States. Their value can often be traced directly to the work of the master – their Scoutmaster.

Sheepshank

Knot tying has long been synonymous with Scouting, just as fire building, hiking or the Good Turn. A Scout's first experience with tying Tenderfoot knots is more like a game. He learns to work a series of rope puzzles without much thought as to their ultimate use. As he grows in Scouting, he learns the character of each knot...how to tie it, how to untie it and how to apply the knot for its best use. Knot tying becomes rope work and later can be applied in the skills of pioneering.

One of the knots I learned as a Tenderfoot was the Sheepshank. I liked it because of its odd name and because it looked complicated. In reality, it is quite easy to tie.

I'll have to make an honest confession about the Sheepshank. In my many years of camping and Scouting, I have had little use for the Sheepshank. It is a knot used to shorten a length of rope without cutting it. One of its weaknesses is in the fact that for it to work properly, the rope must be kept taunt. If the pressure is slacked, the Sheepshank falls apart.

Contrary to my experiences with rope work, I find that the Sheepshank is a very useful concept in the character development process. If a leader is to effectively influence the character of a young person, he must find and apply methods for shortening the distance between him and the youth...a warm smile, a listening ear, a commitment of time, a genuine personal caring. If tied properly, these knots are most secure when the pressure is on.

If tied by a skilled leader, these knots become acquired skills in the life of a Scout. They touch his character and become a working force for him.

In a way, I really like the Sheepshank. I promise to use it more in the future. How about you?

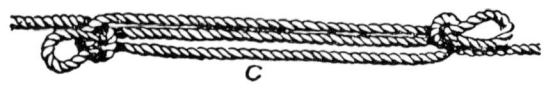

Sheepshank.

14

If You Can Take It

Funny how our roles in life often reverse. When I was a boy, my dad took me to the barber shop regularly. Then, after many years of haircuts on my own, dad reached his 80's and could no longer drive. It become my turn to take him for his hair cuts. I remember well one of those trips when I was the "taker." Having been a barber in his early years, dad could never quite adjust to the thought of a haircut costing over a dollar. He insisted that I find a "dollar barber shop." Surprisingly enough, there was one on a side street downtown. After a friendly greeting and lots of barber talk, Shorty the Barber, launched into his $1.00 routine. No sheep ever had a better shearing...zip up one side and down the other...a dash of tonic...and a once over with the comb to even out what was left. Dad stepped out of the chair, looked at me and said, "Son, do you want a haircut?" I said, "No sir, I just brought you to get one." With that he replied, "Well sit down there. If you think you can take it, I'll pay for it!"

For Scouting to succeed in its mission of developing young people, strong in character, it must rely on both elements...someone to pay for it and someone to take it. Many people help pay for it: the founders of our movement who gave much of their lives for Scouting, the communities who support Scouting through United Way, our Sustaining Members, parents and the Scouts themselves. Anything of value involves a cost to be paid.

Anything of value involves a cost to be paid. But who will take it?

But who will take it? That is the job of the volunteer Scouter today. Many dedicated volunteers have taken Scouting this far. Now it is in our hands to take it to the kids of our generation. The Spirit of Scouting, the values of good character, must be taken to every Den Meeting, Hike, Troop Campout and Explorer Event. A good leader takes it by personal example.

A Scout Salute to Mason

While attending a Camporee last weekend, I met Mason for the first time. He was asleep on the ground outside his tent. In fact, he had to sleep there all night, no cover, no ground cloth, just pine needles and grass. He was not allowed to compete in any of the events and did not get a Camporee Patch.

Yet, when it comes to orientation skills and leadership, Mason can outdo any Scout in the District. Mason is Assistant Scoutmaster Jim Dawkin's new seeing-eye dog. He was already the most popular member of Troop 227 and this was only his first campout with them.

Mason is less than two years old, but with his excellent vision and affection for Jim, he leads him through traffic, around the neighborhood, to work, to church, and of course, on the campouts of Troop 227. What an inspiration it is to see Jim and Mason together!

I see this same relationship developing between Scouts and Scouting. As boys learn to let Scouting lead them, they develop a special vision which is carried throughout life. Scouting helps lead them through hazards, to friendship, to knowledge, to understanding of others and to a recognition of God's power in their lives.

This whole process, of course, depends on leaders who can see in boys the hope of our future...leaders whose vision helps them see beyond sleeping on the ground or receiving a camporee patch.

Ten of What?

In a recent Cub Scout Blue and Gold Banquet, a dad performed numerous magical tricks to the delight and entertainment of Cub Scouts and their families. In the tradition of all good magic acts, the magician called a Cub Scout from the audience to assist in a card trick. After cutting, shuffling, having the Cub pick a card, showing it to the audience, and more cutting and shuffling, the magician went to work trying to identify that card. He supposedly tried mind reading, trick handkerchiefs, secret pockets, and all of the magical powers at his command. It all seemed fruitless. In desperation, he finally asked the Cub what card it was? The conversation went like this: "A ten. A ten of what? I don't know. What color was it? Black. What did it look like?" Then a small girl on the front row held up her hand, showing eagerness to help out her Cub Scout friend. What did it look like? Her reply, "Like puppy prints!" That ended the questions and the card trick, but the laughter rang out for some time after.

Cub Scouting offers parents a special opportunity to help shape the character of their children in that brief period of life which is laced with magic and innocence, a time when the ten of clubs is simply a ten of puppy prints. We all know that as life goes on, we must learn to call a spade a spade and a club a club. Innocence and magic are replaced by stark realities. People who miss the wonderment of youth too often have to face the tough reality of living without those strong friends called imagination and wonder.

Mom or dad, why not get in on the act now? We've identified the card for you, why not play it? Cub Scouting is the game.

Bugler...Sound Off!

A new Scouter in our Council recently visited the office to discuss ways he could best help Scouting as a volunteer. While we were getting acquainted, he was looking over some of the Scouting keepsakes on the walls and shelves of my office. He quickly asked, "Vick, where is your old Scout Bugle? You have Scout hiking sticks, hats, canteens, patches and pictures. What you need is a good ol' beat up brass bugle." As our conversation drifted to more important matters, I forgot the bugle.

Two days later, a completely abused specimen of a Scout Bugle appeared on my desk. I called to thank my friend for his gift, explaining that we needed a good story to go with such a treasure from Scouting's past. The best I could uncover was that the bugle had been used many years ago as a torture instrument to awaken the Scouts from their restful nights in camp.

All of this conjured up in my mind some of the great camp bugler stories from my Scouting years. Bugles stuffed with everything from peanut butter to dirty socks...lost mouthpieces, bugler's alarm clock reprogrammed, buckets of water over doorways, alum in the mouthpiece.

Why is it traditional to hate the bugler? Could it be that he is a symbol of authority telling you what to do and when to do it...wake up, go to sleep, go eat, salute the flag, come to attention. We all have a built-in dislike for sounds of authority, even when they come across in musical notes.

Is all of that dislike real or some of it just traditional? As I remember Scout Camp at Orchard Pond, the bugle calls were something that made camp special. Waking up to reveille was a happy experience because camp days were exciting adventures. The chow call and swim call were announcements of two of the most enjoyable camp events. I remember taps as sort of a prayer set to music for a youngster who was just learning the meaning of prayer.

Please remember, Scouting Leaders, when you sound that note of authority, it may stir some resentment at the time, but it is something all Scouts need. Their understanding and appreciation will grow as they assume roles of authority and responsibility themselves.

Carry A Big Stick?

At our recent Cub Leader's Pow Wow, each faculty member was presented a staff or hiking stick by the course director. In the opening session, participants were told if they had questions regarding schedule or location of teaching areas, just to inquire from one of the Scouters carrying a staff. It so happened, as a courtesy, I was given a staff. During the first break, I was leaning innocently on my staff in the hallway. "Where is the Ceremonies Section?" "What time does the next period start?" "Where can I get my Pow Wow Book punched?" Questions began to come from every side. It was then I decided if I was to be a leader and carry the "big stick" I had better do more than just look like a leader. I got a copy of the program and began to ask some questions myself. Soon, I was an authority on telling people where to go.

One of the truths I try to share with every new Eagle Scout, is that the Eagle Badge marks him as a leader. He is expected to know more, do more, and be more than the average Scout. The Eagle is not a badge of authority, but a badge of responsibility and service.

What badge do you wear in Scouting? Is it just a nice, polished staff to lean on or does it say to the youth of our movement, "Here is someone I can count on." His commitment is to caring and serving. If we wear the badge, we should not be surprised that more is expected of us.

Goodwill

Last week, I met with a group of United Way agency directors. In a discussion, someone asked the director of Goodwill Industries for her business card. The card created laughs around the table as the director explained the message it carried.

It was a rather typical business card...proper form, Goodwill logo, address and telephone number of Goodwill Industries. But, the message read, "Isn't that Suit You're Wearing Ready for Goodwill?"

Sometimes I wish my Scouting business card carried a similar message. Once in awhile, I meet a Scouter who seems to have just been tapped out for membership in the Order of the "Sparrow." He or she seems to pick up every little problem and toss it upon the wind to find a nest in someone's hair. They have forgotten their capacity to love others, to forgive others, and to help others. They have built their nest in a "me tree."

The business card I imagine sharing with them would look something like this: Big smiling face of a Cub Scout in the upper right hand corner. Under him, the words "A Cub Scout Gives Goodwill." Printed across the rest of the card: "Isn't that Uniform you're Wearing Ready for some Goodwill?" If the uniform fits...well, you know the rest.

Rare, Medium or Well Done?

A Dad recently told about his young son and several friends building a club house in the backyard. Of course, to be a real club house it had to have rules. His son explained, "There are three rules: (1) Don't act big, (2) Don't act Little, (3) Act medium." Now these aren't bad rules for any club, any church, any family, any nation. When you think about them, they are the essence of the Scout Oath and Law. Don't Act Big. Don't act too big for God...A Scout is Reverent. Don't act too big for Others...Help other people at all times. Don't act too big for your britches...To keep myself physically strong, mentally awake and morally straight. Don't Act Too Little. A Scout is Brave...A Scout is Obedient...A Scout is Helpful, Act Medium. What is medium? I think about the little signs they stick up in steaks at some restaurants. They say well done, rare, medium well, medium or some other term of "doneness." You can't always go by the sign, however. The proof is in the tasting. What is it like on the inside?

A medium person is one who has a taste of kindness and compassion. One who has been tried in the heat long enough to stand the heat and gain flavor and character as a result of it. He does not think himself too little or too big to love and share with others. I'll take mine, Medium.

Hooked and didn't know it

I read a news article recently from Rochester, Minn. It told of a lady who backed her car from a parking lot at a local hospital and drove about three miles. She became very concerned in that a small car was following her at every turn. She stopped in a service station to get help. Upon examination, she reported to police this incredible story...she had accidently hooked her trailer hitch under the bumper of a small car and towed it away with her.

Every good Scout leader has had a similar experience. One day you discover a small boy making every turn which you make. He walks like you, talks like you, and tries in every way to be like you. You just accidentally, before you realized it, attached yourself to a young person. This special attachment is a part of the magic of Scouting.

What a challenging responsibility. May God give us the wisdom and courage to lead them in paths of righteousness.

"Poison Ivy, Easy to Spot"

For the past several days we have been exposed to some "clever" editorial comments by some of our more noted news writers as they have tried to convince us that another cherished institution in America has "gone to the dogs" because it changed its identifying logo to SCOUTING U.S.A.

They would have everyone believe that Scouting no longer represents values in which we can trust. According to these editorialists, the change is almost like a hangman's knot with which we have executed most of what is good and right about Scouting.

I think America needs to hear from those who are daily involved in the challenge to help her youth learn and, accept as their own, the moral values which give meaning to life.

We need to listen to the Cub Scout leader who meets every week in her home with eight to ten of someone else's kids to help them learn respect for God and Country and to accept responsibility. We need to listen to the Scoutmaster tell us why he takes his time, spends his money and often sacrifices his vacation to take his Troop of Scouts to summer camp.

How sad it is that, all too many, people in our country have been programmed to seek out the negatives. Recently, I was showing a group of parents a slide story of our new Scout Camp. The pictures and narrative portrayed the exciting adventure and beauty which awaits those who will be camping there. After the showing, one parent came to me and said, "You had better check those slides before you show them again. The very first one shows poison ivy growing up that tree where the camp sign is."

I wonder how, in the midst of all the exciting and positive images of the new camp, could one's primary observation have been the poison ivy?

Of course there's poison ivy at camp! In fact, there's a little bit of poison ivy growing in all of us. One of the greater values young people can learn in Scouting is to identify the good and to seek out the best in others.

The One Channel

Cable TV is finally coming to our community. This event has created a great deal of discussion regarding the pros and cons of TV. One mother's evaluation was recently published in our local newspaper. Her family subscribed to cable TV a few weeks ago. She told how she had anticipated being able to satisfy her every entertainment desire by turning through the multiple channels until she reached just the right one. Now that she has the service, she finds that it has captured her entire family. They are all turning the multiple channels, and most of the time, watching programs just because they are there. She explained how her family has lost nearly all of their meaningful time together.

This mother's comments presents a rather accurate diagnosis of a more serious malady which has infected much of family life today. Science and technology has produced endless "channels" from which to choose in trying to entertain ourselves. We are caught up in tuning from one to another, and finally we settle on something which is less than satisfying.

Have you discovered the secret channel? It is the one channel which can ultimately satisfy. It is not one of the in-coming channels. It is that unique out-going channel of service to others. By tuning to it we can get caught up in the satisfying experience of making life better for others. Scouting is a rather unique network which communicates through this channel of service. You can help parents and kids "tune in." Invite someone to join Scouting today.

CHAPTER TWO

Signs of Life

Breathe Normally   26

On Falling   27

Important Measurements   28

Mistakes We Can't Cover   29

The Heart Of A Friend   30

Pitching In The Dark   31

Ever Make A Heart Map?   32

Hidden Power   33

The Breath of Life   34

The Living Circle   35

Learning The "Together Stroke"   36

Up Is Different From Down   37

New Snakebite Treatment   38

Breathe Normally

On a recent airline flight, for some reason, I consciously listened to the emergency instructions given by the stewardess. Having been exposed to this information countless times, I somehow had the feeling that I could give the instructions myself in case of stewardess failure. This time, as I received and stored each bit of emergency advice, I actually heard her say, "In the unlikely event of cabin depressurization, the oxygen mask will drop down. Pull it over your head and breathe normally." Breathe Normally? Did I hear her correctly? Please tell me, who breathes normally in an unlikely event of a little air turbulence, much less cabin depressurization?

In today's turbulent society, we are faced daily with emergencies which call for our best in values, skills and leadership. We get many conflicting emergency messages telling us how to respond. Most of the time, we just close our minds to these confusing signals and simply hope for the best. This works well until the worst happens...our cabin depressurizes. The prospects can be life-threatening unless, somehow, we have on board those qualities of character which automatically drop down before us and become our life support system.

The mission statement of the Boy Scouts of America reads: "It is the mission of the Boy Scouts of America to serve others by helping instill values in young people and in other ways prepare them to make ethical choices over their lifetime in achieving their full potential."

With this mission before us, Scouting cannot afford to breathe normally. Our heart rate must be stirred by the wave of our Flag, the Tenderfoot Scout repeating the Scout Oath and the Cub Scout's closing prayer. Does the business of equipping youth with values for a lifetime excite you? If it does, you are a true Scouter.

May you never breathe normally in these exciting times.

On Falling

One morning last week, I walked into the conference room at the Boy Scout Office and discovered our large decorative Golden Eagle had fallen from over the fireplace and was lying on the hearth. Investigation revealed that the hanger had pulled from the wall during the night. The Eagle had a crack across the back and a couple of small feathers were broken off. Considering the fall, he was in good shape. Back in place now, you would hardly know our Eagle had fallen.

On the same day, I was helping a visitor look through the Book of Eagles to find the picture and biography of a young friend who achieved Eagle in 1974. As I turned the pages and looked at the pictures of hundreds of young Eagle Scouts of past years, I began to wonder how many of them have fallen? Surely at some stage in life they will have taken a fall. Often those falls will result from their attaching themselves to something that "pulls loose in the night."

More important than whether they fall is, how well they recover. When I saw our decorative Eagle lying on the hearth, I thought surely it must have broken into a hundred pieces. I found, however, it was not made, as I had suspected, with plaster, but with tough fiberglass.

In a fall, it is fiber that holds us together. Scouting seeks to build those fibers into every Eagle and into every Scout who aspires to Eagle. Those fibers may be as simple as a good turn or as universal as seeing God in a sunrise, but together they make him tough in a fall.

Important Measurements

Scouting has long been recognized as a character building program. On Beaver Day at Camp Montgomery, six Scouters found themselves in a distinctively different building program. We were building a latrine. Our building crew included two professional cabinet makers, a camp ranger, an ice cream maker, a District Executive and a Council Scout Executive. The cabinet makers measured the lumber in dimensions to the nearest 1/8 inch. Then it was handed to the cutting crew. We ripped it off to the nearest nail-scored mark with a chain saw. This gross disregard for precision created considerable discussion as the latrine building took shape.

One of the professional cabinet makers likened us to the apprentice he had working in his shop. He told how one day the boy was seen carefully walking across the shop, elbows bent, hands extended forward at chest level with palms facing. He stopped the boy to ask him something and was quickly told, "Don't bother me now, I am carrying an important measurement." To all future Scout Campers who enjoy the comforts of Mountain View latrine, we hope you will be forgiving of the mis-measured scars of hammer and saw created by the unprofessional latrine builders. After all, the cabinet makers forgave us after they couldn't change us.

Have you ever considered the important measurements we give to boys in Scouting? We give them codes and promises by which they can measure their actions. If we are wise, we also give them examples from which they can take measurements to carry with them in life. When a Scout stands with his hands in the Scout Sign, there are three important measurements indicated: from hand to head, from head to heart and heart back to hand. He learns to say the Oath. He thinks about its meaning. He accepts it as a part of his being, and finally he puts hand and heart to the task of living it.

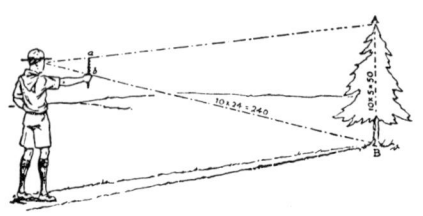

Mistakes We Can't Cover

Last spring when key Scouting representatives met at the state capitol to present the annual Report To The Governor, I joined a group of Cub Scouts in touring our beautiful capitol building. We were invited to view a slide presentation depicting the historical design and construction of the Arkansas state capitol building.

There are many interesting stories surrounding the capitol construction, but one was especially intriguing to me. The capitol was built on the site of the old state prison. In fact, it was built inside the old state prison walls. When the foundation was laid out, the builder oriented it on a North/South line. He assumed that Capitol Avenue ran due East and West. The error did not become evident until the prison wall was later torn down revealing that the building had been built several degrees off square from the avenue. The front walk from Capitol Avenue today has a large angle in it to allow it to connect with the capitol steps.

Scouting has its strongest influence on young people at the time when they are laying foundations and deciding on the orientation for their lives. This key process is subject to serious error if it takes place behind a wall. Scouting helps tear down those walls whether they be social, economic, racial or religious. People cannot learn to relate to people unless there is a freedom of association and an exchange of respect and friendship.

Twice in the past week, I was contacted by young Eagle Scouts. One came with a deep concern for his young friend who had recently attempted suicide. How could he help? What could he say or do? The second called to ask how he could help a young Second Class Scout who had failed his Board of Review three times.

What caused this orientation toward helping other people in the lives of these young men? Could it be their foundation? Was it laid in the open, caring spirit of Scouting?

The Heart of A Friend

The news today carried an amazing story of a 14-year-old girl whose life was saved by her 15-year-old friend. This was not a swimming rescue, emergency first aid or a daring feat of heroic action which avoided death. As a matter of fact, it involved death...death of the lad who saved his friend. He gave her his heart.

Personal Health

The young girl was dying with a heart problem and doctors were seeking a compatible heart for transplant. The young boy told his parents that if he died, he would like for his heart to go to his friend. Within 24 hours the boy died from the rupture of blood vessels in his brain. His heart was transplanted into the girl...a perfectly matched and compatible heart. She is living today with the heart of a friend.

One strange aspect of this life saving story was the fact that both of these children lived in a very small town. There was no nation-wide search for a heart. It was close by in the body of a friend.

Scouting touches daily the lives of unnumbered kids who have heart problems. The flow of love is scarce to none. The chambers are void of any respect for God. The heart muscles has been weakened by the lack of self esteem and the exercise of service to others.

Their best hope is that there is someone right in their own town who has a heart which is strong and compatible, but more importantly, one who has the courage and compassion to share their heart. It will not cost you your death, but it will cost a part of your life. Scouting deals with heart issues. Take a look at your heart. Is it compatible to the needs of kids? Are you willing to share it, even to save one?

I often talk with Scouts who are now men. They tell me how they are living with the heart of a friend, their Scoutmaster.

Pitching in the Dark

Recently, a Scout Dad who is an Assistant Scoutmaster, was lamenting a strange practice of his Troop. It seems that they always pitch their tents in the dark. On backpacking trips when it appears logical to stop and make camp in late afternoon, they seem driven to get in that last mile or two before dark. He says their Troop is getting good at pitching in the dark for they get constant practice.

His lament reminded me of my Eagle Scout friend Jim Dawkins and his instructions to his Troop..."Be sure to bring your flashlights in case we get into camp after dark. If you forget, see me, I'll show you how to put up a tent in the dark. I'm a specialist." Eagle Jim has been blind from birth, but he has a special light which illuminates all of us who know and love him.

How many times have you pitched your tent in the dark? As I review life, it seems that it has been a constant process for me. The Bible calls it walking in faith. That doesn't mean we thoughtlessly pitch in a dry gully which may become a raging torrent with the first rain or pitch under a dead pine which could turn into a dead-fall with the first wind storm.

Scouting teaches a boy to choose a proper site for pitching his tent. With his light he looks above. He looks around. He looks down. He does all of this even when pitching after dark. He learns to exercise his best training and skills...those taught him by his leader, who truly cares where his boys pitch their tents.

Ever Make A Heart Map?

On the wall above our breakfast table hangs a unique map. It is a map of the United States with small hearts placed across it in special locations. Those heart spots range from Florida to California with several designations in between. This rather ordinary United States Map has become special to Anne and me. The hearts we have placed there designate the towns where our children and their families now live.

The skills of mapping were a part of those I learned as a 12 year-old in my efforts to become a First Class Scout...how to orient a map, read map symbols, determine distances, and locate a route or direction to be followed. Had my parents made a heart map at that time, it would have been quite simple...just a few hearts clustered around a northwest Florida town. But, that soon changed. Their map expanded to include a little-known place called New Guinea in the southwest Pacific where my brother was called to serve in World War II.

My early Scout training provided me with the basic skills of mapping and, in ways which I did not understand, helped me to begin identifying some of the important symbols on the heart map. A much deeper understanding came when I entered the heart-intensive responsibility known as parenting.

I learned that it is very difficult to orient the heart map. You always want to tilt it back toward you, forgetting true north. Even though the symbols for those new towns are the same as the symbols for your own town, you can never believe that they are as safe, clean or caring as were you live. You understand what the scale of miles means but you find it hard to accept the fact that the ones you love are miles from you. So, how do you locate the best route and the direction you should follow when the heart map is stretched out before you?

It all must begin with teaching your children those mapping fundamentals. Teach them that God is the true north by which all of their maps can be faithfully oriented. Let them sense the magnetic orientation of family love which can span great distances, leap high mountains, and even reach to low places. This orientation must take place when all of the hearts are together. If it happens there, then neither height nor depth nor space will ever truly separate us from those we love.

Scouting gives us a special place to work on that orientation at a time when many hearts are together.

Hidden Power

Over the past several months I have made many trips along U.S. Highway 65 to the location of our new Scout Camp. Each trip takes me past a small inconspicuous sign with the numerals 374-5 painted on it. The sign marks the entrance to a narrow road leading about 100 yards east of the highway where a grey metal mound rests in a cluster of antenna near the center of a pasture. Cows graze peacefully around this "374-5."

It is impossible for me to comprehend the forces which lie hidden beneath this peaceful landscape. The missile buried there hundreds of feet below the ground has the force and capability to fly thousands of miles and rain complete destruction on several cities with its multiple warheads. With this awesome power, it is designed to deter those who might choose to destroy us.

Just a few miles further along Highway 65, I reach another small inconspicuous sign which reads, "Cove Creek Scout Reservation." A narrow dirt road there leads to a beautiful area of hills, trees and streams with small clusters of tents where boys and their leaders are camping.

Here too, I find it impossible to comprehend the power which lies buried in the minds and hearts of those young Scouts who camp there. In them lies the power of God to heal, to mend, to help, to care, to share and to make peace.

When I travel the road to Scout Camp and see the enthusiasm of youth and the dedication of their leaders, I realize that HERE is where we must uncover and activate the hidden power if 374-5 is to remain buried forever in its peaceful pasture.

The Breath of Life

In a recent meeting of the National Court of Honor of the Boy Scouts of America, we witnessed the presentation of the Medal of Honor to a 15 year old Scout for his heroism and Scout action in the rescue of a friend from the raging waters of a drainage ditch.

The most amazing element of this rescue was the fact that the victim was entangled in wire and trapped under water. For fifteen minutes the Scout took air to him and kept him alive by breathing into his mouth.

This very exceptional and heroic act by a Scout reminds me of the more common and daily acts of our unsung heroes...those adult Scouting leaders who day by day continue to breathe into America's youth the basic moral values of respect for God and Country, and concern for fellowman.

These "acts" must continue, for they are the breath of life which keeps our nation alive. Character and Leadership...what America needs most, Scouting helps build.

The Living Circle

The Living Circle is a familiar scene to all who have been a part of Cub Scouting. It is made by a group of Cub Scouts standing in a circle with their left hand extended toward the center. Each one grasps the thumb of the Cub Scout to his left and extends his thumb for the Cub on his right to grasp. Together their hands form a complete circle. With their right hands they give the Cub sign and then pledge to "Do Our Best."

Last night, I was helping organize a new Cub Scout Den and for a closing ceremony I showed the Cubs (and one younger sister) how to form the Living Circle. As I looked down on the circle of hands, I thought how out-of-place my big hand seems among ten little ones.

Later as I drove home, I remembered the first Living Circle I joined in...it was 1940. As a Den Chief, I was asked to teach our Cubs how to form the Living Circle. In the 38 years since then, I have learned that Scouting itself IS a Living Circle.

God has given to us in Scouting the privilege of joining hands with the finest people of our land...people who care about people. Every time an adult Scouter puts his hand and his heart into helping young people, he is joining that Living Circle. I am convinced that one of Scouting's unique privileges is that of placing our larger hand in with the smaller ones.

Thank God for the Living Circle of Scouting.

Learning the Together Stroke

A Scouting friend recently sent me a story titled, "My Son Beside Me." It is an account of courage and inspiration. A sixty-four-year old man was endeavoring to become the oldest man to swim the English Channel. He had failed the year before. This time, he swam for over 12 hours.

The tides were driving him off course. Night had fallen. The cold was penetrating. It looked as if, once again, he had lost his battle. His son, who was in the attending rescue boat, jumped into the water to assist in rescue if needed. Harper said afterward, "And I knew that with my son beside me, I was going to make it." He did make it. Thirteen hours and fifty-two minutes after he left the shore of England, he staggered ashore in France, the oldest person to swim the English Channel.

This reminded me of the words of my dear wife, Anne, when we were suffering through the loss of our oldest son. She said, "For many years now our family has needed us; at this time we very much need them." Yes, we all need one another. Young people need adults who are ready to jump in and swim with them when they are struggling in life's tides. But, we adults need children who will swim beside us. A look into their faces, the sound of their voices, the inspiration of their youthful spirit gives us that extra something we need to win life's battles, regardless of our age.

Let's all work harder on becoming encouragers to those who swim against life's tides.

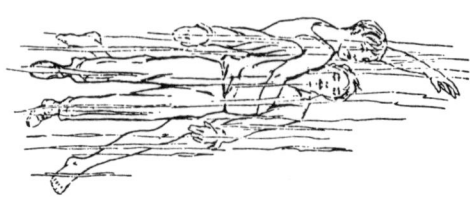

Up is Different From Down

When Skylab was being built the scientists and engineers decided, that in order to save vital space, they should put the various control panels around the interior of the ship with no regard for floor/ceiling or top/bottom orientation. Their reasoning was...that in weightlessness the up and down positions were not important. The experience of the astronauts who lived and worked in the Skylab environment, however, proved the opposite. They reported that even as they floated in weightlessness, they found it necessary to establish a mental orientation of up and down, top and bottom.

In today's "earth lab" young people often find themselves in weightlessness...just floating, with no moral orientation for right and wrong, good and bad. Those who wish to manipulate the lives of young people seek to place these controls out of their reach.

Scouting has recognized from its beginning that young people must have moral values built into their lives by adults who believe in them and who are willing to help them discover values.

As Scouters, our function is that of human engineers who help decide the placement of those moral control panels...Duty to God, Service to Others. We must help assure that in every Scouting activity the "control panels" are there and within reach.

New Snake Bite Treatment

In a recent Commissioners' Conference, I listened to a very moving story of how a dad treated his son's snake bite. The dad is a Webelos Den Leader. He was not a first aid instructor who was telling us about ice packs, constriction bands and hurry cases. He is a dad whose values have been dramatically changed by a copperhead bite which his son suffered several months ago.

This dad told us how he stood by his son as he lay on a stretcher in the emergency room. He said that the eight short years of his son's life flashed through his mind like an accelerated movie. He didn't like what he saw. He realized that dad had not been a main character in many of the important scenes. Right then, he determined, "If my boy lives, I am going to get involved with him in the things that count." He went on to say, "That is why, today my son and I are enjoying the Webelos Program together and we plan to move on into Scouting together."

Why wait for a snake bite, Dad and Mom! Let's begin the treatment today. Your son grows a day, every day, whether you do anything with him or not.

CHAPTER THREE

Nature's Signs

Hind

DEER MOUSE

CROW

DUCK

Does This Rock Your Conscience? 40

Sure Is A Good Day To Make A Garden 41

On "Seeds" 42

Love The Wild Mulberries 43

Whistle While You Work 44

A Pigeon Scout 45

How Many Feathers Does A Seagull Have? 46

Let's Celebrate 47

The Middle Tree 48

You Can Be A Giant Killer 49

If The Creek Don't Rise 50

Does This Rock Your Conscience?

This summer, I made a long anticipated trip to the Petrified Forest National Park in Arizona. I had heard descriptions of the amazing "rock wood" and had seen samples of the multi-colored rocks formed from the ageless trees, but I was not mentally prepared to deal with the two-hundred million year old statement. I was having trouble just comprehending the fact that 1984 was already half over. When the Park Ranger explained that these trees were two-hundred million years old, it overloaded my circuits. So, I immediately began shifting to something within the range of my comprehension.

I looked into a display case labeled Conscience Rocks. There were stones of various sizes and each had a note or a letter attached. Some were typed formally and others hand written on scraps of paper. The message of each was basically the same..."I am returning this rock I picked up in the park. I know it was against the rules. When the Ranger at the gate asked if I was taking anything from the Park, I replied no. I know it was wrong, so I am returning this rock to get it off my conscience." Now, that, I can comprehend.

When I was in the third grade, I took a clean, white piece of chalk off of the school chalk board. That afternoon when I got home with it, my mother asked, "Where did you get that?" I tried to explain, but while I was trying, she was packing me in the car, driving me back to school and instructing me to take that chalk back to the 3rd grade room and put it on the chalk ledge from where I had taken it.

I'm not wise enough to explain just what conscience is or where it comes from, but one thing I do know is that our conscience is molded in the hands of those who love us: Parents, Scout Leaders, Teachers, Religious Leaders, and of course, Our Heavenly Father.

On My Honor—

Sure Is A Good Day To Make A Garden

Over the past two weekends, I have enjoyed visiting several District Camporees across the Council. The spring days have been perfect with warm sunshine, cool breezes and the fresh smells of springtime. What a perfect time for camping out with your buddies and competing in the skills of Scouting.

As I stood by observing one Troop preparing their supper, I struck up a conversation with the Scoutmaster. We both agreed it had been a near perfect day...when he said, "It sure would have been a good day to make a garden." I knew what he meant, for that morning while driving out to the Camporee, I had seen many folks "hard at" the job of making their garden.

As I drove home that evening, I realized that many Scouting leaders had missed this near perfect day to make a garden, or, had they? I think not.

You see, at these Spring Camporees I saw the most productive and valuable gardens in America being cultivated and planted. I saw the fertile minds of our youth being prepared for the seeds of Respect, Concern for Others, Patriotism, and Love for God. I saw teamwork, friendship, courtesy, kindness, and reverence growing. Of course, they weren't planted in straight rows, for character can never be planted that way. It is sown, some here and some there, one seed at a time by the example and deed of a leader who cares about the way kids grow up.

Thank you Scouters, those who took these warm perfect days to lead your boys at the Camporee. Indeed you help make a grand garden, and America will enjoy the fruits of it.

Gardening

On Seeds

When I returned from a Camporee yesterday, I noticed that I had picked up quite a few beggarweed seeds on my trouser legs. As I sat picking them off, I began thinking about all of the unique and subtle ways God has devised to scatter the seeds of nature...they "beg" a ride on your trousers or in the hair of an animal, they drift on the wind, they "explode" from the pod, they entice man and beast to carry them away for food. Some species of pine seed, I understand, remain closed in their cone for years until a wood fire triggers them to open and scatter.

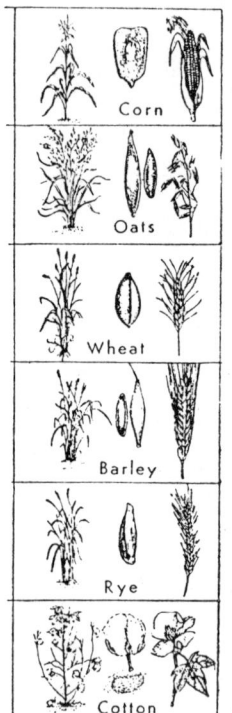

As I thought back to the Camporee, I realized that God has also devised some rather unique means of scattering His love. I had observed the seeds of respect, loyalty, reverence, friendliness, helpfulness and kindness being scattered in the fertile lives of youth by a group of adult leaders whom God has chosen as His sowers.

Some of these seeds stick to the Scouts and may go unnoticed for a long time. Some are picked up and carried away because they are packaged as attractive and tasty to kids. Some will lie dormant for years until there is an emergency in the boy's life and then they will come out to grow and give new life.

Thank God for His unique ways of planting His seeds within us.

Love The Wild Mulberries

Last evening, I was talking with a friend about growing fruit trees. He was lamenting the fact that his two cherry trees loaded with fruit had been systematically unloaded by his feathered friends. If that were not enough, he said, "Have I told you about my fig tree?" I waited for his second sad story. It seems that several years ago, his brother gave him a sprout from a fig tree. He planted it and then replanted it through two family moves. He watered it and nurtured it to a large healthy tree, but no figs came forth in response to his care. This spring a friend looked at his tree and said, "Harold, that ain't no fig. You've got a wild mulberry there." What a let down for an amateur nurseryman. In disgust, he cut down his mulberry tree.

When Scout Leaders and parents start out with a Tiger Cub or a Tenderfoot, we always have in our minds that vision of a handsome Eagle Scout prepared in mind and body for every challenge in life. We plant, water and nurture through the growing seasons as well as the droughts, all of the time anticipating the best fruits. Often, we find that young person growing into the type of leader we dreamed of. Many times, however, instead of an Eagle, we get a Second Class; instead of a Senior Patrol Leader, a Quartermaster of the Wild Skunk Patrol.

Don't cut that wild mulberry down. Think of the shade it produces, the food for birds and small animals and the nesting place for God's creatures.

He gave us our young people. Let's dream dreams for them, nurture them and see in them God's gifts even when they don't fit the dreams we planted. Let's love them for who they are. Who knows, someday they may invent the "Mulberry Newton!"

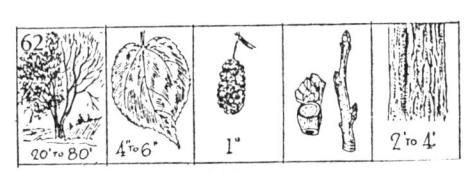

Mulberry

Whistle While You Work

Did you know that during World War I, messenger pigeons were a key resource in American front line communications? I read recently that they were so effective in getting messages past enemy lines, that the German Army eventually trained hawks to attack these pigeons and bring them down. Americans then learned that they could protect the pigeons against hawk attacks by attaching small whistles to each bird. The flight of the bird created a constant sounding of the whistle which frightened off the hawks. The effective communications continued.

During World War I, Scouting was in its infancy, but it was already finding ways to communicate the important messages of character, service and physical fitness to the youth of that day. Scouts were taught to help old ladies across the street, stop runaway horses, kill mad dogs, and revive drowning victims with the "back pressure arm lift" method. The drug problem they faced was dealt with in a simple paragraph in their handbook titled, "Whether to Drink Coffee and Tea." Discovery and technology have made most of these methods and techniques obsolete, but Scouting is constantly discovering new ways to communicate the skills of living to America's youth. The spirit and values of Scouting remain constant in face of those who seek to attack them and bring them down.

You see, we have discovered that by attaching special little devices like Bobcat, Webelos, Tenderfoot, and Eagle, we can create a "new sound" in a young person which becomes a life-long deterrent to those forces which attack their character and values.

Remember, we can't fly their mission for them, but through Scouting, we can protect their flight.

A Pigeon Scout?

Several days ago I was standing across the street from the Federal Building waiting for a friend. It was a rainy morning and people were scurrying to keep out of the rain. As I cast my "weather eye" to the sky, I happened to notice one of the large stone Eagles right under the peak of the building. His stern and imposing features portraying strength and majesty, immediately identified him as the emblem of our nation, the American Eagle.

There was another bird in this scene, however. His presence and position prompted me to share these thoughts with you. Perched directly on top of our Eagle's head was a pigeon. You see, he had found himself a dry, comfortable and protected place.

A few days after this bird watching episode, I was invited to participate in a Court of Honor recognizing a new Eagle Scout. The bird scene immediately came back to me and the accompanying thought that there is no such thing as a "Pigeon Scout."

Scouting seeks to develop young people who are a credit to our nation and who are willing to give back to her their strength, courage and honor. These are the qualities of the Eagle, and these are the same qualities for which Scouting awards its highest rank.

America doesn't need any more "pigeons" who are just looking for protection and security, who never do anything to help preserve it, and who "fly away" as soon as the weather changes. No, I do not think there will ever be a "Pigeon Scout Award."

How Many Feathers Does A Sea Gull Have?

This question was asked me recently by a six-year-old. How would you have answered him? The best I could come up with was: "No one knows, because sea gulls get very mad when you start counting their feathers."

This very simple question has stimulated my thinking relative to the most basic concern of a sea gull..."Will it Fly?" Not how many feathers, but will it fly?

It seems that we are too prone today to ask questions like: "How many advancements did you have? How many boys are in your Pack? How many Scouts attended the Camporee? Or, how many leaders attended the training session?

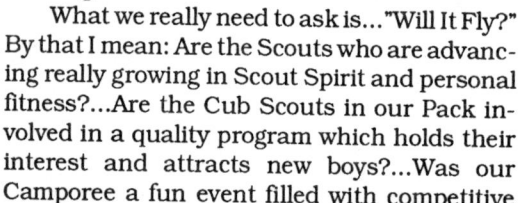

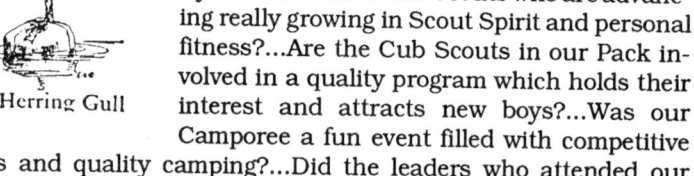

Herring Gull

What we really need to ask is..."Will It Fly?" By that I mean: Are the Scouts who are advancing really growing in Scout Spirit and personal fitness?...Are the Cub Scouts in our Pack involved in a quality program which holds their interest and attracts new boys?...Was our Camporee a fun event filled with competitive skills and quality camping?...Did the leaders who attended our training event come away with a new dedication and a bag of skills to make Scouting real for those who joined with high expectations?

Let's ask ourselves, not how many feathers, but will it fly?

Let's Celebrate

On March 15, in Hinckley, Ohio, over 25,000 persons gathered to celebrate the annual return of the buzzards. Legend has it that the buzzards have returned to Hinckley from Florida each spring for the past 99 years. The Chamber of Commerce sponsors an annual $3.00 per plate pancake breakfast to celebrate the event.

Of course, this celebration is a spoof to raise money and bring attention to a small and otherwise little noticed community, yet it reminds me that "celebrating the buzzards" has become quite popular in many segments of society today. One of the most certain ways to draw a crowd is to exploit that which is rotten or stinks. Just rate it with an "X" or label it "for the mature" and it will surely attract flocks to feed on filth.

Soon after I read about the buzzard celebration, I was invited to participate in a Court of Honor recognizing four young men as new Eagle Scouts. There were approximately thirty-five persons who attended this celebration. It attracted Scout Leaders, Sunday School teachers, brothers, sisters, fellow Scouts, grandparents, and proud parents. They came to celebrate with these Eagle Scouts their discovery of that which is good, alive and worthy of the name Eagle.

If we are truly looking for something to celebrate, let's praise God and give thanks for young people who are feeding and growing on the values expressed in the Scout Oath and Law. Scouting gives us much to celebrate.

The Middle Tree

Did these peaches come off of the middle tree?

On a recent visit to the farmer's market, I overheard a lady asking that question of a farmer. He assured her that his peaches were definitely from the middle tree and their quality was the highest.

I didn't stop to check further his endorsement of quality, but in my mind's eye, I could see his orchard of many average peach trees, with a central tree rising above all the rest, its leaves greener, trunk stronger, peaches larger and tastier than all the rest. That seems to be the image he was selling.

Your council has just completed a very successful summer season of Cub/Dads, Troop Camps, Day Camps and Explorer Events. In all of these activities, it was evident that some Cubs, Scouts, and Explorers come from the "Middle Tree." Their enthusiasm, skills and appearance all gave evidence to the quality of the units they represent. You see these "middle tree" Packs, Troops and Posts provide young people with programs and committed adult leaders who live out the principles of Scouting. The strong evidence is that they usually produce the "pick of the crop." Could the young people in your unit be recognized as coming from the "Middle Tree?"

You Can Become A Giant Killer

The world truly has some big problems to solve today. It is easy for us to become defeated by those "giants" whether real or imagined.

A recent news article told of a peach farmer whose orchard was very near a nuclear generating plant. He complained, that since the plant began operation, his peach trees have been less productive and many are dead or dying. His implication was that the nuclear plant must be ruining his peaches.

The nuclear generating company called in some of the nation's best known peach specialists to examine the problem and determine the cause. After extensive study of the trees, soil, air, water and radiation levels, the scientists came to the following conclusion: the decline in the orchard is the result of poor cultivation practices and a resulting deterioration in the quality of the soil in which the trees are grown.

Fruit Culture

It would be very easy to blame a decline in our Pack, Troop or Post on such giants as: more competition for kid's time, not enough leaders, lack of parents who care, lack of respect, and discipline.

If we are honest with ourselves and the young people we serve, we must admit that when we work at the job of cultivating strong leaders, exciting programs, and high moral values, Scouting will continue to produce a crop of future citizens of which our nation can be proud.

If The Creek Don't Rise...

A good friend of mine suggested that sometime I write a story expressing my views regarding the ol' sayin', "If the Creek Don't Rise." His suggestion was timely. It came right after a downpour at Cove Creek Scout Reservation. The Creek was over the entrance road and we were expecting three hundred Cub Scouts and Dads to arrive shortly.

Well, personally, I don't like the sayin', "If the Creek Don't Rise." What kind of commitment is that? Scouting would be in bad shape if we only had people who could be counted on when the creeks don't rise. Not very many kids would get a chance to be Scouts and those who did would have a very dull experience.

Good Scouters operate under the theme, "Since the Creeks Do Rise." The shortened version of that is, "Be Prepared." We all know that life is full of creeks that rise and we prepare for high water. First, with a positive attitude, then with a "go get a boat" spirit. We don't whine about being wet. We talk about how great it will be when the water goes down.

Scouting has not reached over sixty million young people in America by operating under the reserve clause, "If the Creek Don't Rise." This strong and positive force for God and our Country has been carried forth to youth by men and women who work at it, to borrow another "ol' sayin,' "Come Hell or High Water."

CHAPTER FOUR

Signs of The Times

Blacksmithing

Space Exploration

Happy New Year   52

Prepared For Today   53

A Backward Glance   54

I Can't Say It   55

It Can't Be Unstuffed   56

Getting On To The Good Part   57

Letter From A Clown   58

Not Without Getting Wet   59

The Three Boys   60

The Eight Minute Mile   61

No Scaled Down Version   62

Well Done   63

Full Service Management   64

On Mixing Cement   65

Time Release   66

Happy New Year

Today is January 6th. Over the past several days, nearly every personal contact has been punctuated with the greeting, "Happy New Year," followed by the anticipated, "Happy New Year to You." The appropriateness of New Year's well-wishing seems to overshadow the more common "How ya doin?" or other every-day greetings.

What do we really mean with our greeting, "Happy New Year?" I can't speak for you, but I have tried to evaluate the New Year's wish from the perspective of a Scout.

Happy...a very important word to him. Happiness, better known to a boy as fun, constitutes his primary goal when becoming a Scout. Fun is the key ingredient of the promises made by his Scout Handbook and by the boys who have been Scouts before him. Happy new years are made of happy days, and happy days are created from fun-filled moments...hiking, camping, swimming, eating.

New...the word itself stirs excitement. Adults are excited by things like new cars, new jobs, new friends, new clothes. How much more is that 8-year-old or 11-year-old excited about flying a new kite, making a new friend, camping in a new spot, or catching a new fish. His having so many new things to see, and try, makes it nearly impossible for those of us who are less than new to keep up with him.

Year...Don't talk to him about a year. What's happening today, right now? I once met with a brand new Troop of Scouts to tell them about the fun they should expect of Scouting. In the meeting, I showed them a set of Scout badges from Tenderfoot to Eagle. One of the Scouts I knew well. His father is an Eagle. I said, "Ralph, when you earn your Eagle, will you let me present it?" He replied, "If you are still living then." Time for boys can better be measured in minutes than in weeks, months or years.

Happy New Year can be more than a wish for your Scouts. As a leader, you have that special power to make their wishes come true. Happy New Year to you all.

Prepared For Today

If you were a new Scout in 1911 and wanted to know how to live up to the Scout Motto, "Be Prepared," you could have turned to page 260 of your Boy Scout Handbook and read the latest and most effective methods for stopping runaway horses and mad dogs. Included in the instructions are such heroics as "running along side the wagon, seizing the reins and turning the horse toward a wall or house." Directions for stopping a mad dog were a bit more daring. You accomplished this by "wrapping your coat around your left arm, letting the dog bite it, then seizing the dog's throat with your other hand and choking him." This hands-on approach seems quite amusing to a Scout today who lives in a world relatively free of mad dogs and runaway horses.

Scouting has recently launched a new preparedness program for youth titled "Prepared for Today." It's key element is a guide for adults to use in helping children think and talk through the proper responses to problems and emergencies which they face in today's world. The mad dogs and runaway horses are still on the streets, but they have taken on new names...pushers, pimps, punks and pornographers...to name a few.

How will our children ever learn to stop these animals unless we take time to help them Prepare for Today. Instructions in a book will do little to help. Parents and leaders who love and care enough for our children can help them learn to cope. Best of all, in the process of preparing, children come out feeling good about themselves.

Scout protecting child from mad dog

A Backward Glance

Recently, while waiting for a Scouting appointment in an auto dealership, I inquired as to where I might find the men's washroom. A salesman directed me out to the service area, where I found a grease-ladened door marked MEN. The interior design measured up to the best in blue-collar washrooms...lava soap, institutional towel rolls with no take-up reel, empty Air Wick bottle, plumbers friend with broken handle, and a bare 25-watt bulb with hex-nut pull string. The most striking and unusual piece of decor was the washroom mirror. It was functional, yet it carried the design and motif of the establishment. It was a rear view mirror from an automobile.

Most of us could do without the other accessories I mentioned but somehow, I think, it would be most beneficial if we each kept a "rear view mirror" handy for some daily reflections.

Some people advise, "never look back," but I recommend occasional backward looks to enhance our vision of the present and into the future. Consider how soon we, in Scouting, would become blind leaders of youth if we forgot to look back at the Duty to God and Service to Others concepts which were laid in the foundations of our movement. Every meeting which is opened with the Scout Oath, Cub Promise, or Explorer Code does, in fact, provide youth with a glance backward and a strong look forward. A good backward glance reminds us that blessings we have today are most often the gifts of sacrifice made by those who came before us. It reminds us that "new" is not necessarily better or even best.

For a clearer vision of the future I recommend "the rear view mirror" as standard equipment on all models: Cubs, Scouts, Explorers and, most of all, their Leaders.

"I Can't Say It"

In a Cub Scout Blue and Gold Banquet we were all standing at attention as the Color Guard entered with the Flag. Tiger Cubs in their orange shirts, Cubs in their blue and gold uniforms, Webelos in their distinctive plaid neckerchiefs, parents and the younger brothers and sisters wearing their proud smiles.

"Will you join me in the Pledge to the Flag?" The Webelos Scout could not have said it with more authority and command had he been a member of the Presidential Honor Guard. We all began together, "I Pledge Allegiance to the Flag of the United States of America"...Shattering those stirring words came a cry of despair..."I can't say it, I can't say it." A Tiger Cub's little brother who wanted more than anything else to be like his Tiger brother just couldn't put all of those very important words together. He was heart broken..."I can't say it, I can't say it."

What this little boy did not realize was that at one time in our lives, every person in that room, "couldn't say it." But, we all had parents, teachers, big brothers, sisters and Scouting leaders who loved us enough to teach us how to say it. Surely this little boy, whether he knew it or not, was about to experience that same sharing love.

The real despairing cry today comes from those young people who won't say it, who do not know it, and who understand nothing of its meaning. We see them at sports events and public gatherings. No one ever loved them enough to help them discover a sense of pride and respect for our Nation and our Flag. They have been nurtured on the negatives. They have been told most often, what's wrong with America.

Let's hear their cry and redouble our efforts to bring every kid possible into Scouting where they are nourished on the principles of Duty to God and Country. The most loving thing we can do for America is to teach her children to love her and respect her.

It Can't Be Unstuffed

An ol' timer and Sea Scout friend of mine was great at spinning yarns both on land and on sea. Some of his best stories came from his memories of his college days. This was one of his most memorable.

It seems that the mascot of his college was an owl named Sammy. He was five feet tall, made of fabric and stuffed with straw. On the eve of a big football game with their college arch-rivals, a raiding party relieved them of mascot Sammy. Their college Rally Club set out to rescue Sammy from the rivals before he could become a part of their pep rally bonfire.

The now-famous rescue, according to my friend, included a sneak foray into the rival's field house, a chase over and through a string of freight cars, commandeering of the train by the Rally Club, and a 100 mile train chase from one city to another. When the train ran out of water and stopped, the Rally Club members jumped from the engine and ran through the woods carrying their beloved Sammy. The rivals were hot on their heels, and about to recapture Sammy. Somewhere in the woods Sammy's protectors unstuffed him, folded his cloth hide and carried him out of the woods unnoticed in their overalls. Of course, the tale has a happy ending. The rescuers arrived just in time for their own pep rally and bonfire with "unstuffed" Sammy safe and secure.

In the enjoyment of retelling my friend's famous rescue story, it occurred to me that every Scout faces times in his life when he would like to be able to unstuff himself and just fade unnoticed into the woods. A personal commitment to the principles of the Scout Oath and Law does not always place us in a popular stance. A stand for personal integrity can cost one friendships. A commitment to mental and moral fitness can be a lonely road. The practice of Duty to God can, in some groups, elicit taunts and ridicule. But, a good Scout knows that filling his life with those values which Scouting teaches gives him a strong measure of the Right Stuff...the stuff that becomes part of his very fabric. It cannot be unstuffed at will. Sorry 'bout that, Sammy!

**BE PREPARED
TO HELP OTHER PEOPLE
AT ALL TIMES**

Getting On To The Good Part

On a recent visit with our six-year-old granddaughter and her parents, we were experiencing the trauma of a rainy Saturday afternoon where all were shut in against our wishes. The TV had been on for much too long when mother of the household pushed the "off" button, saying, "That's enough. Go find something else to do." Sensing the clouds now gathering inside, I said, "Blythe, go get a book and I'll read you a story." With a smile, she soon returned saying, "This is the one, Grampa. Read me this one." What is the name of it Blythe? *Where Did I Come From?* I could see the rest of the family standing in the kitchen snickering just a bit, but I accepted my responsibilities...just read it as if it were Mickey Mouse.

Well, it started out like Mother Goose. Page one...a picture of a stork flying with a baby hanging by his diaper. "Maybe someone told you the stork brought you." Next page...Mother and baby in hospital bed..."Maybe someone told you mother found you at the hospital." With that, Blythe took the book and said, "Grampa, skip all of that stuff and let's get over there to the good part." Mother Goose's gynecologist could not have explained it better. Each part and participle led us to that final statement, "Now you know where you came from." That was an understatement!

I remember as a boy my favorite book was my Boy Scout Handbook. It began with the Scout Oath and Law, the Good Turn, and the Motto. Those basics were required. My Scoutmaster told me I had to learn them. My personal preference however, was to skip them and get on over to the good part...camping out, hiking, building fires, reading a compass, saving a life.

My years in Scouting have taught me that you really can't separate the mission of Scouting into good parts, unimportant parts, or boring parts. Its message is not, Where I Came From, but Where I Can Go, What I Can Become. When a young person discovers the answers to those questions, he has surely found that "good part."

Letter From a Clown

Our granddaughter, Blythe, will be five this month. She has always had a special friend at our house, a clown her grandmother made when Blythe was two. Not only is he a friend, he is a doctor. His clown name originally was Bubbles, but after he helped Blythe, her dolls and bears, through several bouts with ear infections, he became, Dr. Bubbles.

Two years ago, Blythe and her parents moved to Kansas. It seemed a shame that she might lose touch with a friend who cared so much for her. Dr. Bubbles agreed, with my help, to write Blythe a picture letter every week telling of his adventures, discoveries and sometimes even his troubles. (Clowns have those, too.)

It is surprising how much one can learn from helping a clown write letters to a 5-year-old. No matter how serious a predicament he might get into, (he calls them boo boos) he always has the ability to turn them into a laugh. His life and discoveries somehow, paralleled those of Blythe's. In a sense, they are growing up together and letting me share in it.

DR. BUBBLES

How thankful we must be in Scouting that we can share that growing up process with our children. With a little love and imagination, we can help them turn their boo boos into smiles and laughs.

One day when I was talking with Blythe on the phone, I told her about a letter Dr. Bubbles had just written. She said, "But you helped him, didn't you, Grandpa?" Yes, we have to help our children learn to laugh, and love and live. When we get caught up in providing the "things" they need, we often fail to take time to share the best life has to give...our love. We are prone to take ourselves and our problems too seriously.

One thing I have noticed about the adults in Scouting...in it all, we have preserved some of the joys of youth and we keep them alive by sharing them with our children. Thanks, Dr. Bubbles.

Not Without Getting Wet

Have you heard about the Scout who was turned down on his swimming merit badge? He showed up at the waterfront in a new pair of designer swim trunks. He had memorized the seven requirements for earning the badge. He knew the safety rules. He could describe all of the body coordination involved in the backstroke, breaststroke, crawl and trudgen. But, when the instructor asked him to get into the water and demonstrate these skills, his reply was, "I didn't know it involved that. I don't believe in getting wet."

Vick, you ask, did that really happen? Well, of course not. But you probably heard what did happen...A Scout came before his Board of Review for the Life Scout Award. He had the proper merit badges and skill awards. He had served the proper time limits in some leadership role in his Troop. In Troop meetings, Courts of Honor, and other Scout functions, he had regularly raised his hand to the Scout Sign and said, "On my honor, I will do my best to do my duty to God..." But when the Review Committee asked him to explain what Duty to God means in his life, he said, "I don't believe in God, so I didn't think that applied to me."

A Scout cannot earn a swimming merit badge without getting wet. A Scout cannot earn the Life Award without a personal commitment to the Duty to God concept of Scouting.

Do the Scouts in your Troop have a regular association with that concept through your example and through activities designed to make them aware of God in their life? A recognition of this fundamental value must be cultivated long before the Scout reaches his Life Review.

The "Three" Boys

When was the last time you played, "Three Bears?" Well, I'll have to admit, last Saturday was the first time I had played "Three Bears" in a long, long time. Michael, my four-year-old neighbor, came to the fence while I was raking leaves and asked, "Will you play Three Bears with me?" To be honest, I had a lot more leaves to rake and some Razorbacks, not Bears, who were to play that afternoon.

Does an adult really have time to play Three Bears with a four-year-old? A moments hesitation was all that he needed. Over the fence Michael came and began explaining how it was with the Three Bears. Michael told me all about the porridge that was in the bowls, how the chairs were set and three beds. He pointed to them right there behind the shrubs.

He said, "Now let's go for a walk in the woods and see what happens." He took my hand as we started for a long walk around the yard, but when we neared the "Bear's House" again, he turned loose of my hand and said, "You don't need to hold my hand now we are nearly home."

In that Saturday afternoon game, I got reacquainted with the Three Bears, but more importantly, I gained a fresh understanding of the Three Boys...One who needs so badly an adult to share some time with him...One who needs an adult by his side to give him a hand in strange territory...and One who needs an adult who understands there is a time to turn loose and let him walk on his own.

Scouting gives adults an opportunity to be important in the lives of these "Three Boys." Look and you may find them most anywhere...on your street, in your yard, or even in your house.

The Eight Minute Mile

Last week at the start of the 71st Anniversary Scout Parade, I was standing on the steps of the State Capitol. At that moment, units of several hundred Scouts assembled down town, were stepping off of their mile-long parade route to the Capitol.

Two mothers of Cub Scouts came up to me and asked, "How long will it take them to get here...about 8 minutes?" I said, "No mam, it will take close to 45 minutes." One mother replied, "That's what I get for listening to an 8-year-old."

How time flies when you are having fun! We all know that times means very little to youngsters. They figure they have a whole lifetime of it so why sweat it. As parents and leaders who have a view from this end of the parade, we realize that they will get here all too soon.

Scouting gives us one of our best opportunities to help them develop a cadence, follow the leader, carry their flag proudly, and demonstrate the spirit of Scouting.

Let's keep the Scouting parade going. The age of youth is a very short time in which we have an opportunity to share life's most important values with them. Take time to enjoy it.

No Scaled Down Version

Several years ago, I was driving home from an Executive Board Meeting with a rather wealthy Board Member and Scouter. I had often thought that his strong interest in Scouting would someday lead him to make a significant gift to the Council Trust Fund.

The subject of boats came up as we traveled and he began telling me about a large sailboat a friend had built and given to him. He said it was too large for him to keep and he would like to give it to Scouting...that is, if we thought we could use it. Visions of sugarplums began to dance in my head, for I knew we had several Sea Explorer Ships which could make good use of such a craft.

When we arrived at his home, he said, "Wait here a minute and I'll go get that boat for you." In a moment, he appeared back at the car carrying a large ship model of the Cutty Sark. Have you ever tried cleaning melted sugarplums out of your car? That sailboat gift still graces the top of a cabinet in my office. It regularly reminds me of unmet expectations.

I have often thought that every Scouting leader should have hanging prominently in view, a slightly used uniform or a hardly opened handbook to remind us that boys dream big dreams about Scouting and we must not be guilty of giving them some scaled-down version which looks okay but doesn't offer the promised adventures.

Well Done!

One of the most remarkable and inspiring leaders in the Boy Scouts of America lives and serves right here in the Quapaw Area Council...Mr. E. A. Bowen, serving youth as Scoutmaster of Troop 24, Asbury United Methodist Church, for the past 55 years. We all stand awed in the shadow of this great Scouter's faithful tenure and service to boys.

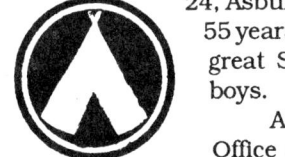

Camping

A friend recently brought to the Scout Office some old issues of Scouting Magazine. I delight in reading old handbooks and literature from Scouting's past, so the magazines did not lie unopened for long. I had turned only a few pages in a July, 1936, issue when from this forty-two year old magazine, there appeared some of the early footprints of Scoutmaster Bowen...an article he had written, to share with the Scoutmasters of America and titled, Some Objectives of Camping.

Though the message had been folded away in the yellowed pages of this magazine for the lifetime of many of us, I cannot think of a more up-to-date and relevant statement on camping for today's Scoutmaster...Mr. Bowen says, "Camping is one of the phases of Scouting which a leader cannot afford to omit from his program. It is so important in the estimation of boys and in the development of the Troop morale that it should receive a generous portion of the time allotted to the Troop. If camping is well done, no other activity pays higher dividends."

Is camping in your Troop "Well Done" or "Medium Rare?"

Full Service Management

There is a service station near my house with a large sign out front which reads, "Under New Management." The paint on the sign is peeling. This is to be expected, for the sign has been hanging there day and night for the past two years.

On my desk this morning is a letter from an Eagle Scout expressing his disappointment that Scouting has become too "city" oriented with not enough "out-of-doors." Regularly, I hear from Scouts and leaders who express the feeling that "new" is not as good as "old." They ask with concern, "Why did they change the awards requirements? Why the new name? Why is Exploring co-ed? Why build a new camp? Why the change in Uniforms?"

It is my strong belief, that Scouting is just as new or just as old as the managers make it. And, who are the managers?

They are the volunteer leaders. You manage the quality of the program which reaches the young people in your Pack, Troop or Post. It depends on your personal commitment of time, skills and example, not on a handbook or a new set of requirements.

Next to the new management sign at the service station is another sign which makes the first completely irrelevant. It reads "Self Service." In one sense, Scouting never has been, nor will it ever be, Self Service. Young people learn a respect for God, the joy of serving others, and the skills of leadership from the example and service of their volunteer leaders.

Scout Masters' Manual

A handbook especially prepared to aid the scout master in his work with boys.

It is full of suggestions!

Programs for Scout Meetings; indoors and out, summer and winter; long term camp, Scout games, etc.

Price 60 cents postpaid

National Headquarters
200 Fifth Avenue   New York, N. Y.

"On Mixing Cement"

Last week I was walking in the neighborhood early one morning when I noticed something strange...the sidewalk had a band-aid on it. Not one which had been discarded, but one neatly attached across a crack in the cement. Now, this really wasn't too strange if you know the tough bunch of kids who live in the house there. I smiled as I walked on and said to myself, "One of them probably fell there and instead of the kid getting hurt, they had to bandage up the sidewalk."

That reminded me of the old sayin' which goes something like this, "We all live with our nose to the grindstone. Whether it grinds us down or polishes us up depends on what we are made of." Scouting leaders have a unique opportunity to sift and mix the ingredients which ultimately solidify into the character of a young person.

Cement Work

Scouting offers a tough mixture compounded to withstand life's tests. Mix it well, pour it into a boy-shaped mold and it will soon harden into a man.

Time Release

Remember those "tiny time capsules" and how the modern medicine men tell us they "burst forth" periodically in our bodies providing healing medication as we need it.

What an ingenious device...an automatic time-release designed to work within us apart from our conscience effort.

Did you know that Scouting developed the tiny time capsule long before modern medicine men came up with their 24-hour concoctions. I talk with men nearly every day who tell me how, some quality of character learned years ago as a part of the Scout Oath and Law, suddenly and automatically releases itself and strongly influences the direction of their lives.

Scouting still needs "medicine men and women" who can put together these life values and hide them away in the lives of youth for future release. This exciting reality should activate the chemistry in each of us to share the best of life with our young people.

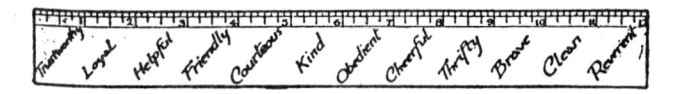

Requirement No. 12
"Furnish satisfactory evidence that he has put into practice in his daily life the principles of the Scout Oath and Law."

CHAPTER FIVE
Danger Signs

A Rescue Knot   68

Someone Removed The Stop Sign   69

Weather People   70

Warnings, Dangers And Risks   71

Automatic Bailers   72

When The Heat Is On   73

In A Hole?   74

The 13th Floor   75

A Little Explosive Properly Applied   76

Implosion   77

Let's Make A Point   78

Could You Be Last?   79

Protection That Lasts   80

A Rescue Knot

Recently I had one of the most enjoyable experiences which Scouting affords. I helped organize a new Scout Troop. In our first meeting with a group of enthusiastic eleven-year-old Scout candidates, we were teaching them some of the skills of ropework. Beginning with a few simple knots, we worked our way up to the bowline, a basic rescue knot. We demonstrated how, tied around the waist, the bowline can help save a life. It can be used for pulling a person in, lifting them up, or letting them down to a place of safety.

One of the Scouts who quickly mastered the bowline was very insistent on leaving his rope tied around his waist. When asked about taking it off to practice other knots, he said, "No, I want to leave it on to show my mom when I get home."

I wonder how enthusiasticly Mom responded to the bowline her son had learned to tie. Did she take time to listen to him? Did she say," son, I am proud of you?" I wonder if maybe she even let him teach her how to tie a bowline?

A good parent must know how to tie a few knots. The basic ones are called, "I love you, knot," "Let's try this together, knot," and "I'm proud of you, knot." These, too, are rescue knots used to lift your child to a new level of self worth. All are worth learning to tie. Let's practice them with our kids.

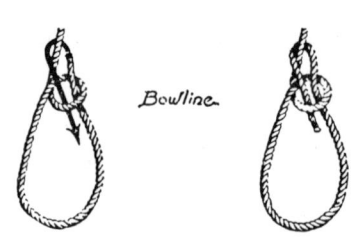

Bowline

Someone Removed the STOP Sign

A recent news article carried a picture of a sign being placed at an intersection. It read,, "A young man's life was lost here because someone removed the STOP sign." The story related how vandals had been stealing STOP signs in the area. A young driver had driven into the intersection where a sign was missing. He lost his life in the resulting auto crash.

An appeal was made to those who may be stealing the signs as "souvenirs" for their rooms. "Please consider the tragic consequences and return the signs."

There seems to be a world-wide epidemic of removing STOP signs. It often goes unnoticed under the guise of "new morality," "individual rights," or "doing my thing." The inevitable crashes which result bring needless human suffering and remorse.

Scouting has the rewarding and positive task of putting up signs along those streets and intersections most heavily traveled by young people. Scouting's signs say, "GO!" Go fishing, go camping, go hiking, go do a Good Turn, go help someone, go serve God and Country.

How are we doing with our sign business? Do we understand this as the heart and purpose of every hike, den meeting, Court of Honor, or camp out? Have we noticed that WE are the signs they read best? It's not enough for us to read to them. They must see us living by these signs of life. Look!...There is a young person approaching your intersection now? "Sign's up!"

Weather People

Have you ever thought of yourself as a weather person? As we move through this season of tornados and thunderstorms, it seems that few evenings go by without some indicator of watch or warning being trailed across the bottom of our TV screen. They just suddenly appear there, oblivious to the love scene, nature scene or moment of drama which they might invade. They seem so impersonal, yet their intent is so very personal. YOU may be in danger! YOU need to be aware! YOU need to act!

In a sense, every good Scout Leader is a weather person. We have weathered life, endured its storms of loss and disappointment, lived out the dark nights and warmed again in the morning sunshine of the new days given us.

In our hands has been placed that unique responsibility for the preparations and broadcast of those watches and warnings which can guard or save lives of our youth. Consider for a moment, your Scout may have tuned in his widescreen to a full-color view of his favorite camping spot. What a great place for your message to enter. "This is the world God has made. You are it's keeper. Take care of it and love it."

In another drama scene, some Scout has violated his honor by cheating or lying or stealing. Over this whole bad scene, a quiet message can be displayed by the good weather person, "God created us to love and help one another. I love you, and I want to help you. Trust me."

The on-going tragic drama of drugs is being tuned in by many young sets today. Could it be one of yours? Your message trails quietly across his screen, "God created you, He loves you. Protect that wonderful gift of life that is in you. Don't let it be stolen from you."

In the growing-up years, storms can do their greatest damage. While young people are enjoying the sunshine, we can serve them well by observing life's weather patterns and issuing a watch or warning when needed.

FAIR WEATHER   RAIN or SNOW   LOCAL RAIN or SNOW.   TEMPERATURE·   COLD WAVE

Warnings, Dangers and Risks

From my office window, I can see a freshly posted billboard advertising a popular brand of cigarettes. About six square feet of the sign is devoted to the message, "The Surgeon General has determined that cigarette smoking is dangerous to your health." The remainder of the board seeks to convey the pleasurable aspects of smoking. It must be irritating to the cigarette companies to have to post this warning with their otherwise appeal-oriented message.

It is just human nature for us to want to hear the good message and not be confronted with warnings, risks and dangers. Yet, whether we heed them or not, every important choice in life is accompanied by warnings and risks.

In an old printing of the Scout Handbook, there is a chapter on trail signs. It is surprising how many of them relate to warnings...Dangers, Bad Water, Dangerous Animal, etc. The fact is that all of life's trails can be better traveled when we are alert to the dangers and risks. Scouting provides adults a special opportunity to make young people aware of these risks when they are making life's choices.

There has never been a perfect hike or expedition, but the very best ones are made by those who are prepared in mind, body and spirit. We should all take satisfaction in the fact that Scouting's appeal for fun and adventure carries with it the admonition, "Be Prepared."

Automatic Bailers

Time spent aboard my sail boat, riding free on the wind, affords me some of my best thinking time. If you are not a sailor, you may not be familiar with automatic bailers. They are actually holes in the bottom of the boat. Of course, they are more than that. They have an arrangement which allows them to be opened or closed. They are directed so that when the boat is moving briskly through the water, a suction will be created to draw water out of your boat, thus "automatic bailing." But beware, when you are just sitting at the dock, the bailers must be closed! Water will fill your boat through the open bailers and soon sink you. As someone has said, "It is not all the water on the outside that sinks you, it is the water inside the boat."

Occasionally, I hear someone saying Scouting is sinking or Scouting is dying in our Troop or Pack or Community. Then I look around and see great programs in Packs, Troops, and Communities with kids and their parents and leaders enjoying this special time together. What is the difference? I am convinced that when you are moving, you are going to take on some waves, but the forward motion will draw them out again. It's when you are sitting at the dock complaining about the waves that your boat will gradually fill and sink.

Really those bailers aren't automatic. You have to get underway and get out in the wind and waves to make them work. Sailing is great, but Scouting is one of the greatest voyages a young person and an adult can make together.

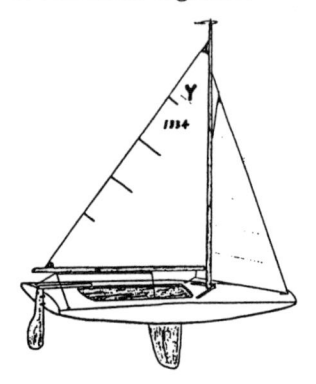

When The Heat Is On

A kindergarten teacher and friend of mine told me last week of a very perceptive youngster in her class named Michael. She had just spent considerable time teaching the kids about the "fireman's roll" and how one can extinguish his burning clothing by rolling over and over, rather than running. She had thoroughly impressed on the children the importance of knowing the technique and remembering to use it in any emergency should their clothing catch fire.

Michael stood up straight and asked permission to speak. He said, "You know, when we die, a lot of us are going to heaven, but

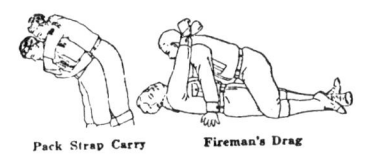

Pack Strap Carry   Fireman's Drag

Fireman's Drag

some are going to the other place and they sure will need to know how to do all that rollin' around."

I'm sure Michael will make a good Scout some day, for he not only learns the lessons of safety quite well, but he believes in application of the Scout motto, Be Prepared.

Seriously, Scouters, when we teach a young person the skills of living, we never know when or how they will be called on to apply them for their own benefit or for the good of others. At the time of learning, the young person may have no stronger motive then to pass a test or just have fun. Those of course, are worthy motives, but, how many times do we hear from former Cubs, Scouts or Explorers who tell us, "When the heat was really on, my Scouting knowledge and leadership skills made the important difference."

Thank you, Scouters, for sharing the best of life with youth!

In A Hole?

Some of my best memories come from the days I spent hunting quail with my dad in the piney woods of north Florida. There were few fences and mostly flat, wooded areas of long-leaf pine and scrub oak. Dad's Model A Ford was built just right to straddle the stumps and high grass as we drove along following the bird dogs in their search for a covey.

One day just at dusk, the two front wheels of his Ford dropped into a deep hole as we drove through a patch of high grass. This had happened before, so, with the axe from the front floorboard, we cut a pine pole and pried the front of the car up enough to back out. It wasn't all that easy, but experience helped.

Automobiling

When we looked up, we discovered the dogs had pointed near where we were retrieving the car. We grabbed our guns, shot the covey, and in haste began to put away the guns, shells and dogs. It was near dusk and past time to be leaving the woods; so, with a quick start, Dad's Ford made its second trip into the same hole! With a look that only my Dad could give, he said, "Don't say a word, just get that pole and start prying." Armed with even more experience, we now got the car out in record time.

All was quiet as we drove on back toward home. Then, Dad broke the silence with this sound advice, "And, you don't have to say a word about this to your mama." I knew what he meant. That sealed my lips until many years later when we were all able to laugh together.

I learned from those hunting trips with my Dad that we all run into holes and we need to be prepared to get ourselves out. It usually isn't as difficult as we think. Use good judgement. Recognize when we are wrong. Never think we are too big to apologize. I learned, too, that it is pretty dumb to run into the same hole twice. You feel embarrassed, and you really don't want others to know about it.

Scouting is a great proving ground where we can run into holes, learn how to get out, and best of all...learn how to keep out!

The 13th Floor

Have you ever occupied a room on the 13th floor of a hotel? Not many people have, for most hotels with thirteen or more floors do not acknowledge the 13th floor. They skip from floor 12 to 14.

On a recent trip, I stayed on the 17th floor of a 25-story hotel. Each time I used the elevator, I noted the absence of floor 13. Why would a hotel go to the trouble and confusion of eliminating one floor from the orderly numerical sequence? The simple answer seems to be that many people are very uncomfortable with the idea of rooming on the 13th floor, even to a point that some refuse.

I guess it is well that we only have twelve points in the Scout Law, for surely there would be those who would be uncomfortable with point 13, whatever character value it might uphold. There might even be those who would refuse to subscribe to it.

A Scoutmaster, of long tenure, recently told me that his biggest challenge was teaching the new Scout how to get along with other people. He said, "Many of them come to me with the attitude that other people are out to 'get' them." Once they begin to learn the meaning of Trustworthy, Loyal, Helpful...they find it more comfortable to trust and share life with friends and fellow Scouts.

It would be quite sad if man succeeded in eliminating all of those things that made him uncomfortable. The grand prize then would be a life that is unthinkably bland and meaningless.

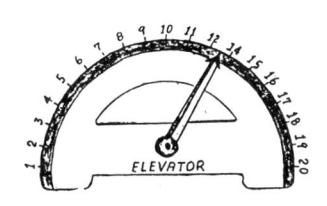

A Little Explosive, Properly Applied

Last week I heard a brief news item which came out of France. Some would-be burglars entered a building by carefully outsmarting two alarm systems. They made their way to the back room which contained the safe. After applying a small quantity of plastic explosive to the safe door, they retreated to the adjoining room to await the small blast. If they had known the potential, they would have retreated to the next block, for the safe was filled with explosives and it blew the whole building down on them.

It is often quite surprising what a little bit of explosive, applied in the right place, can release. Every young person has locked within, a tremendous force for good or for evil, for better or for worse. Scouting leaders have the delicate and challenging task of opening the door just enough and at the right time to release the best that is in a young person.

This release may be accomplished with a small amount of recognition properly applied. It could result from responsibility properly delegated, or the exercise of trust and confidence when there is an important job to be done.

We can't see what is inside of a kid, but we must never be surprised at what he accomplishes when we help him release that potential. Scouting is very explosive that way!

Implosion

Our community has recently experienced an exciting week surrounding the implosion of two landmark hotels to make room for a new Convention Center. The term "implosion" was new to most people around here. We were all familiar with the idea of blowing up a building by exploding it, but the concept of imploding took a little explanation. The experts came on radio and TV telling us that implosion meant placing very small amounts of explosives in key spots to weaken the structure and allow the building to collapse inward. And, that is exactly what they did at 10:41 a.m., Sunday, February 17, 1980. The Marion and Grady Manning Hotels became piles of dust and rubble.

As I thought about the demise of these hotels, I thought also about the many lives which are being "imploded" today. So many young people are being destroyed by a few small charges placed strategically in their moral structure. When the charges are set off, life caves in. Not many lives are blown up. They simply cave in.

It is Scouting's business to defuse these charges and to shore up the character of young people. Each time we help a Scout develop self respect, a care for others, a commitment to God, or allegiance to his Flag and Country, we are strengthening his inner being against whatever charges life may place there.

With Scouting's help, young people have a much better chance of withstanding life's implosions. How rewarding it is to be in the business of building...rather than demolition.

"Let's Make A Point"

During a Junior Leader Training Course held several months ago in another Council, a very strange and near tragic accident occurred. A Scout leaned back against another boy's pack and thought he felt something sharp stick into his back. He was checked at the hospital and nothing found. It later developed that a sewing needle had worked itself into one of his lungs resulting in surgery and his confinement to intensive care. This strange case reminds me of the very positive opportunities Scouting has to assure that many "small character points" are injected into the lives of our Scouts, Cubs, and Explorers on a regular basis.

When leaders make a point of living out the concepts of "Physically strong, Mentally awake and Morally straight," these qualities often enter undetected into the lives of youth. They work their way to the heart and years later, help produce men and women of strong character who care genuinely about the needs of others.

Make it a point this week to share some of the good qualities of life with a young person.

Could You Be Last?

"Man Regrets Roll as End of the Line for His Tribe." This was the headline of a news story which describes the feelings of a 69-year old tribal chief, the last living full-blood male of his tribe. He faces a dilemma in his twilight years. He desperately wants to pass on the heritage of his tribe, but he never learned most of it and has forgotten much of what he did learn. Who could have known 40 or 50 years ago that he would be last?

His mother tried to teach him the language, but managed only to teach him the tribe's burial rites. He memorized them and wrote them down.

There are over four million Scouts and Leaders in America today. Who could ever imagine our "tribe's" being endangered with extinction? But, just for a moment, imagine Scouting with YOU in the role of its last living leader. How well could you pass on the heritage of Scouting? Do you know its language and values well enough to make them exciting and fun for the younger generation? It is of small concern that we remember the requirements for a merit badge, the rules for a Pinewood Derby, or even how to tie a sheepshank. What truly counts is our commitment to pass on to youth the joy of loving and serving God, the satisfaction of serving others, and the peace which comes to a life kept physically strong, mentally awake, and morally straight.

The burial rites are very simple. We don't have to memorize them but they may be important enough for us to write them down and then blot them out. They are only two words...ME FIRST. When consistently applied have the power to kill the Scouting spirit.

The oath and law nourishes that spirit. Kindle it carefully and there will be no end to it.

Protection That Lasts

A few months ago I bought a new pair of running shoes. They were just like the pair I had the year before except this pair rubbed my heel every time I ran. Each morning I would put a Band-aid on my heel. Before I had run the first mile, the Band-aid would have rolled up in a ball just above my shoe top. After several pit stops to replace the Band-aids, I decided there must be a better way. The following morning I placed the Band-aid on my shoe right at the point where it was rubbing. After five months, and many miles of running, that same Band-aid is still in place.

On a recent family camp out with our church Troop, I observed one loving mother advising her new Scout son on how to pitch his tent. Soon our very wise Scoutmaster quietly moved in, took mom by the arm and said, "Hey mom, come on, we have some things to do over here with the adults."

One of the special qualities I have observed in Scouting over the years, is that it encourages us to put the bandages on the right place. As parents, we are prone to want to protect our children from all of life's rubs. We want Band-aids at all of the points of rubbing...disappointments, physical pains, failures, criticism, or having to say, I'm sorry." Scouting gives us the opportunity to put the protection, not on the child, but in the program.

The value system expressed in the Scout Oath and Law, when applied, offers youth a protective edge in dealing with many of life's rubs. Scouting helps protect our children from physical pain by teaching them the buddy system for swimming, to wear life jackets, to fasten seat belts, to practice fire safety, to properly handle a knife and axe and to practice hunter safety. You see, we put the protection in the program. That way, it lasts and lasts. If we put the protection on the kid, he rubs it off and soon throws it away when we are out of sight.

CHAPTER SIX

Trail Signs

Fly Over Or The Right Stuff? 82

Keep 'Em Burning 83

John Jacob Jingleheimer Schmidt 84

Navigational Instincts 85

Leadership...Lost And Found 86

Little Things Communicate 87

Space Listening 88

Feet And Legs 89

A Pain In The Toe 90

What's Cooking? 91

Have You Been Shortsheeted Lately? 92

Scouting Is A Turn Off 93

No Trace 94

Fly Over, Or The Right Stuff?

Over the years as I have been associated with Scouting alumni in churches, civic clubs and business, I find them always ready to reminisce about their Scouting years...the time it snowed 12" on our camp out...the time the raccoons ate all of our food...or the time we got lost for 24 hours. One adventure you can count on, their recalling with a sense of pleasure and achievement, is the Philmont adventure. Any man who, as a youth, hiked the trails of Philmont Scout Ranch in New Mexico, carries with him an inner-sense of pioneer struggle and achievement.

A good Scouter friend just returned from his second trip to Philmont. He recalled, in hushed tones, the scenic beauty of the Sangre De Christo Mountains as seen from the top of Ol' Baldy. In the next breath, he recalled the pain of a man, just slightly out of shape, attempting the climb to the top of Ol' Baldy.

These accounts of pain and pleasure, I have heard many times before from the hikers of the Philmont trails. In fact, my first personal experience with them came in 1954.

What was strikingly different about this Scouter's experience was not his recent trip, but the first Philmont trip he took when he was a boy. He attended an Explorer Conference at Little Rock Air Force Base. One of the highlights of the Conference was an orientation flight in an Air Force plane. That flight turned out to be a fly-over of Philmont Scout Ranch and return to L.R.A.F.B. After only an hour and a half flight...there it was, the Tooth of Time, Ol' Baldy, the Rayado River. Looking down on the whole two-hundred twenty-seven thousand acres, he could only dream about what it must be like to plant your feet on a mountain top, look back on the trail you had been climbing for days and say, "I made it!" Finally, as a man, that dream came true for my friend.

Have you ever wondered how many boys join Scouting and just get a short orientation flight? They read a handbook, join a Patrol, and even go camping, but somehow, never plant their feet on the Scouting trail and start their climb to the mountain tops. How is it in your unit? Just a fly-over, or the right stuff? If we wait until they are men, it may be too late to experience the right stuff!

Keep Em' Burning

Fire by friction has long been one of the more intriguing pioneer skills which challenges the inquisitive and determined Scout. I have long enjoyed the special satisfaction of teaching a Scout to make a bow and drill set and to use it in starting a fire. Usually it comes as a great surprise for him to learn that he does not have to be a real Indian to master the skill.

Last month, I was invited to share this fire building technique with a Troop of thirty Scouts. It was cold outside, but the meeting room temperature climbed as a mass of eager Scouts huddled around my demonstration. Then things really began to heat up!

It was one of those nights. Even though I have taught the skill successfully for many years, nothing went right this time...boards broke, rawhide snapped, spindles jumped out, and sparks faded away before the tinder caught fire.

After much talk about techniques and materials, I realized the bottom line with them was, build a fire! But when? Between the drops of sweat dripping into my glasses, I could see a cloud of doubt gathering over the Scouts.

Finally, one Scout said, "I once read an article about Indians and it said they kept their fires going for days and weeks at a time, only starting a new one when they moved their village or camp." He surmised, "Now I see why they never let their fire go out. It's too hard to start a new one."

Young people come to Scouting with a spirit of enthusiasm, an appetite for adventure, a character which is pliable, a body filled with energy, and a mind seeking answers. If we get too busy to tend these fires and let them die out, who will rekindle them? It is much more satisfying to keep them burning than to try to build anew. Take it from an old fire builder who got a better story than a fire.

"John Jacob Jingleheimer Schmidt"

At Philmont Scout Ranch this summer, we camped with a group of "longtime Scouters." In a songfest one evening, we began reaching back for some ol' time Scout songs. Someone pulled out John Jacob Jingleheimer Schmidt. Do you remember the words?..."That's my name, too. Whenever we go out, the people always shout..John Jacob Jingleheimer Schmidt," and on and on it goes just like "A Hole in the Bottom of the Sea."

Ol' John Jacob was often used as part of a game. One Scout was sent out of the campfire area while everyone agreed on an object that was "it." When the Scout returned, he began his search and all of the others assisted by singing John Jacob Jingleheimer Schmidt to the top of their lungs. The key was to lower the volume as the Scout got near "it" and to raise the volume when he began to wander away from "it." If he listened to Ol' John Jacob, he would soon find "it."

Just a crazy song and a game which provided moments of fun and suspense around many a campfire, but is is not unlike the method a good leader must use in helping Scouts find "it" in life. "It" may be the satisfaction of service to others. "It" may be accepting responsibility for the hard tasks. "It" may be standing up for what is right in the face of criticism. Or, "it" may be confessing a mistake and asking forgiveness.

A good leader knows when a gentle voice is needed and when a loud command will best communicate. He can direct a young Scout's search in life by the quality of signal he transmits.

Navigational Instincts

Scientists have recently discovered that certain microbes have an iron content within them which causes them to line up with the earth's magnetic field. This material, they say, is similar to lodestone.

These microbes, with their built-in orientation, have been found in the heads of pigeons. Some scientists believe that this phenomenon may have some bearing on the homing and navigational instincts of certain animals. A deeper study is underway.

A very close examination of Scouting reveals that there is a character content deep within the program and purpose of the movement. The natural orientation is toward good, not bad...right, not wrong. It is often found only in slight traces and may be undetectable to the Scout in which it grows.

There is overwhelming evidence from the lives of many Scouts, now turned adults, that their Scouting experiences have given them a permanent orientation toward Duty and Honor, God and Country. What greater navigational instinct can we place in the life of a young person?

Leadership...Lost and Found

Several years ago a good friend of mine was serving on a National Jamboree Staff. When his Regional contingent of some 3,000 Scouts assembled and hiked over to the big arena show, Billy was assigned to check the campsite to be sure fires were out and no Scouts were left behind. He was to "bring up the rear" of the 3,000 boy contingent.

At the close of the big show, several hours later, the show marshalls began moving the Regional groups out "on the double," realizing it takes a while to get 3,000 people back to their respective camps. Well, in the process Billy found that he was no longer "bringing" up the rear" but was leading 3,000 boys, hopefully, back to camp! You guessed it, he got 3,000 prople lost in the night at Valley Forge. They hiked 1 1/2 miles "as the drunken crow flies." Billy says "we can all laugh now but it wasn't funny then."

Scouters, have you ever considered that those Scouts who are following you now are one day going to be expected to lead the way, maybe for a family, a church, a business, or even a nation?

We must be faithful to point out to them the land marks and compass readings by which they can lead. We cannot leave it to chance that they will learn a respect for God, a love of our Country, a concern for others, and a deep self-respect. If the leader is lost, how can the followers know their way?

Pathfinding

Little Things Communicate

Last summer I had the privilege of visiting with a friend who had suffered through several years of World War II in a Japanese prison camp. Even as he recounted the experiences, I found it impossible to comprehend the degradation of human spirit which must take place in a prisoner-of-war camp.

I asked him if he and the other prisoners had any way of knowing how the war was progressing during those long months of imprisonment. He said, "Oh yes, that is what kept us alive." He recalled, that with some parts smuggled into the prison camp by Filipinos, one of the American prisoners built a short wave radio inside of a canteen. Each night he listened to the war news broadcast from the west coast of the United States. He then passed that news on through a man-to-man grapevine until every prisoner had received it. In this manner, there was a regular kindling of hope. Communications through a small canteen radio kept alive the spirit of several thousand men.

Often we are prone to discount the value of little things as important communicators. Have you read the Scout Law, The Cub Promise, or the Explorer Code recently? Boys do not learn their meaning by reading them. Truth and meaning are communicated by the little things which they see in the lives of their leaders. They learn about trustworthiness by the way we fulfill our promises. They learn about duty to God by listening for our prayer of thanks at meals or observing how and where we worship God. They learn the importance of keeping one's self "physically strong and mentally awake," by observing how we care for our mind and body. What are we communicating?

These qualities of human spirit are passed on through a man-to-boy chain which is the heart and strength of Scouting.

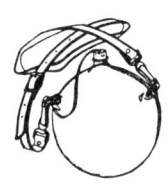

Space Listening

Some of the nation's top scientists are now deeply involved in a project designed to receive messages from deep outer space. They believe that intelligent beings live out there somewhere and that with sophisticated listening devices and abundant patience, we can eventually receive and decipher their radio signals. In fact, we have even directed some messages to "them" and their stars which are 35,000 light years away. All of this presents some rather intriguing thoughts.

But, I'd rather you think with me a minute about the adventures of listening for messages from inner space. There are thousands of emergency messages coming from the hearts of young people every day with far too few receivers positioned properly and tuned in.

Scouting gives adults who care, one of our best opportunities to tune into the inner space and deep concerns of our young people. We are already equipped with the sophisticated instruments...listening ears and caring hearts. Our role as a Scouting Leader puts us in listening positions as advisor, counselor, leader and friend. Young people need answers to their deeper thoughts and good listeners can help them find those answers.

Feet and Legs

On a recent Friday night, I made a list of neglected jobs needing my attention over the weekend. I left the list on the kitchen table where it would be difficult to ignore even on a relaxed Saturday morning. Anne was casually examining the list, I suppose to make sure it included some of her priorities. She let out a squawk when she came to the third item on my list, "Fix Betty's Legs."....What is this all about? The explanation was quite innocent...Some weeks ago, I had agreed to make two new sofa legs to replace broken ones for a friend of ours named Betty. Understand, dear? We had a good laugh and lots of kidding during the day until Betty's legs were fixed.

> **How to Become a Tenderfoot Scout**
>
> "To become a Scout a boy must be at least twelve years of age."
>
> But no boy can be a Scout just because he happens to be old enough. There are also Things he must KNOW and BE.
>
> Most important among these are The Scout Oath and The Scout Law. First a Scout KNOWS them, then the Scout DOES them—that's the way people know he's a Scout—by what he DOES!

Over the years, one of the confusing terms in Scouting has been the plural of Tenderfoot. Leaders often asked me, "Do you call them Tenderfoots or Tenderfeet?" My reply is, "Neither, simply call them Tenderfoot Scouts, and people will understand what you mean." Feet or legs...sometimes our language gets us in trouble.

More important than what you call him...What is a Tenderfoot Scout? I see him as a tender, pliable youngster whose shoes for walking life's trails are not yet broken in. They pinch and rub and often cause pain. So, how does tender become tough? By walking the trail, short sections at a time, and with someone who has been that way before. This is Scouting's method from Tenderfoot to Eagle and from Scribe to Scoutmaster. Learn by doing...teach by example!

Mr. Scoutmaster, why not put on your next "to-do list," "Fix Jimmy's Feet."

"A Pain In The Toe"

Breaking in a new pair of shoes has always been a necessary ordeal for me. Last week, I finally decided it was time to suffer through the break-in period with a new pair which had been challenging me from my closet floor for over a month.

After the first ten minutes, my left little toe was yelling, "Let me out, let me out." In another fifteen minutes, my pain waves had convinced my brain waves that something had to be done. I sat down and took my shoe off. Crammed in a wad around my little toe was something obviously foreign. I unfolded it and this is what I read: "We hope you'll enjoy the comfort, wearability and quality of these shoes that I have inspected, signed, Maeola Little."

This week I had to explain to a Scoutmaster that his 18-year-old Scout was past the age to qualify for Eagle. Occasionally, I have to return tour permit requests where the required safety steps have not been taken. At nearly every Cub Scout Rally, we have to explain to some disappointed youngster why he must wait until he becomes old enough to join. Of course, these cause pain and disappointment, but believe me, the rules of Scouting are not designed for that purpose. Their purpose is to enhance the "comfort, wearability and quality" of Scouting. When they press on your toe, you are prone to think they are out of place.

Please remember, Scouting's purpose is to help build character in people and to develop them physically, mentally and morally. This is an impossible task without the experiencing of some pain.

What's Cookin'?

On a recent radio call-in show the host was interviewing two counselors who work with the shelter program for battered women. They explained the helps which are available to women and to husbands who have the problem of abusing their wives.

At call-in time, the host was confronted by the rather authoritarian voice of an older woman..."I have been married over 40 years and ain't had no batterin' goin on at my house. I don't need no counselor nor no shelter. When my husband gives me trouble I take an iron skillet, heat it hot as I can, lay it up side his head and just peel the skin off. If there's one thing I can't stand, it's violence." Host response, "Lady, I'm glad I don't live at your house."

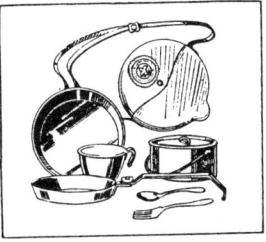

We live in a world where one of the most common responses to problems or frustrations is the iron skillet approach...get em', fight em', hate em', and hit em'. The iron skillet is a very impractical piece of equipment for a Scout. It is too heavy to carry in his pack. It will only serve to cook one dish at a time and is tough to clean up. Scouting designed the aluminum cook kit with folding handle, skillet, pot, lid, plate, cup, and carrying case. It is boy-size and serves his outdoor cooking needs well.

More important than the cook kit, is the Scout approach to problems and frustrations. Scouting gives a boy something that's not too heavy, and it comes in pieces which fit various life needs. We call it the 12 points of the Scout Law, the Cub Scout Promise or the Explorer Code.

Scouting's most important success in cooking comes not as a result of his cook kit, but the master chefs who teach the cookin'!

These are the adults who have spent a lifetime burning things, spilling things and ruining things until they have learned to turn down the heat, follow the recipe, and cook with care.

A Scout Salute to those master chefs who help kids cook up a great dish of fun and character.

Have You Been Short-Sheeted Lately?

While camping at the National Jamboree a few weeks ago, I was awakened by noises outside of my tent. Soon I was overhearing the details of a most sinister plot...one which seems to raise its ugly head every time a group of Scouts camp out, whether it be a 25,000 Scout Jamboree or a Patrol overnighter.

In hushed tones, I heard one Scout say, "Let's short-sheet him." Having often been the victim of such infamous plots, I listened carefully to determine the direction this was to take. I was not ready for the response I heard from the co-conspirator. "Come on, you nut! You can't short-sheet a guy in a sleeping bag!"

As I lay there comfortable and safe in my sleeping bag, I chuckled a bit and soon my thoughts turned to a much larger and more serious plot...those conspirators who are out to "shortsheet" young people with drugs, pornography, Satan worship, and a thousand other forms of deceit and self-destruction.

Can you really short-sheet a guy in a sleeping bag? Well, I guess someone could figure out a way, but generally, it's a safe bet that the short-sheeters are going to look for easier prey.

Scouting does build into youth those qualities which help them stand up to the con-artists who are out to short-sheet their values, their health and their service to mankind. Character development is a serious game and it demands the strongest efforts of those who would serve God through helping young people grow physically strong, mentally awake and morally straight.

Are we giving our best to this cause? The short-sheeters are.

"Scouting Is A Turn Off"

When I was driving on a recent trip, I heard over my car radio a comment which stirred a whole new channel of possibilities in my mind. The speaker said, "Life today for many people, is like watching TV...they don't like what they are watching but they are too lazy to get up and turn it off."

So much has been said and written recently about the low-grade carnal appeal of some of today's TV programming. Laws for control have been proposed, product boycotts threatened, moral surveys conducted and sermons preached to focus concern on those lowest of human values, sometimes fostered under the banner of TV entertainment.

Those degrading values were not discovered by TV. They are as old as life. There has always been that segment of humanity willing to sit by and have garbage dumped on them, yet too lazy to get up and turn it off.

Have you ever stopped to think how Scouting teaches kids to change channels in life? Every merit badge, every den meeting, every hike and every venture of a young person into career exploration is a new channel of positive values.

Scouting gets kids out of their chairs, out into the beauty of God's world. Scouting presents young people live actors who have chosen strong moral values for their life style. They are adults who have the dedication and life commitment to get up and change the channels for our young people.

What a positive force...these volunteer Scouting leaders. I'm glad you are one of them.

No Trace

Glancing out my office window, I caught the full view of a multi-colored bus waiting at the stop light. The rainbow sign arched across its side proclaimed it to be the traveling home of a rock & roll band. As this rolling pot of gold accelerated from the light through a cloud of smoke and oil, I could barely read a message on its rear..."We are a Hard Act to Follow!"

I'm confident the band intended their "final words" to be a positive affirmation of their quality performances. In reality, they expressed the annoyance and exasperation of all motorists and pedestrians who were following in their cloud of noxious gasses.

I recently viewed a slide program prepared by an Eagle Scout. He titled it No Trace Camping. What a great idea...leave all our trails and campsites as if we had never been there. No trace, just nature as God left it for our inspiration and pleasure. We have all seen campsites like the smoking bus, "a hard act to follow." Tin cans, garbage, fire pits, ditches, hacked trees and defaced facilities. Who would ever want to hike or camp there? I challenge every Scout and leader to practice No Trace Camping.

The Eagle Scout closed by reminding us that wilderness survival once meant man's ability to survive the wilderness. Today it means the ability of our wilderness areas to survive man's carelessness. A "No Trace Camper" is truly " a great act to follow."

"Send It On"

Has the message and spirit of Scouting been communicated for you in the parables of **Signs Up**?

Then, why not be a "sender" of that message and spirit? Order, for your Scouting friends, personal gift copies of **Signs Up**.

Use the order form on the reverse side of this page. A card acknowledging your gift will, on request, be shipped with their copy of **Sign's Up**.

It's a "good sign" when we pass to others the spirit of Scouting.

Order Form

Vick Vickery
Good Sign Publishing
4195 April Road
Pensacola, Florida 32504

Please send me _____ copies of
Sign's Up @ 6.95　　　　　　　　　　Amt. $_____
(prices effective through 12/31/96)

plus shipping & handling　　　　　　　　$ 2.50

Enclosed check or money order:　　　　Total $_____

Ordered by:

Name:_____
Address: _____
_____ Zip:_____

Please Ship book to:

Name:_____
Address: _____
_____ Zip:_____

Name:_____
Address: _____
_____ Zip:_____

☐ Please send an acknowledgement card with books shipped.